About the Authors

Alice and Maddie's love of plants started at an early age. They helped their Opa (a Dutch grower of cut flowers) on his nurseries and allotment, and their Mum (an award-winning horticulturist) in the garden and with her cut flower business. Living in a London home with limited outdoor space, they began experimenting with indoor plants before opening their first houseplant shop, Forest, in 2013. Since their first book *The Green Indoors* was published, they have hosted a houseplant show-stand at the Royal Horticultural Society Chelsea Flower Show and have continued to expand and develop their knowledge into the wonderful world of houseplants. As a family, the future is exciting, Forest is continuing to develop, and the sisters are beginning to grow their own houseplants to sell in the shop from the family's new flower farm in Kent.

Maddie Bailey

Maddie began working at Forest in 2013 after school. Inspired by her mother's love for horticulture and the surrounding environment of both houseplants and cut flowers, she began studying horticulture with the RHS in 2015.

After finishing her studies, she continued to work both in the shop and as a gardener. During this time, she expanded her knowledge with self-study and wrote articles for her Instagram account @Muddy_Maddie. The articles combined her love for horticulture, the great outdoors, houseplants and science.

After juggling gardening and shop work for two years, Maddie then travelled around the world to destinations such as South America, the Middle East and the Arctic Circle, taking time to observe plants in different climates and paying particular attention to the plants we cultivate for indoor use.

Alice Bailey

Alice started working at her Mum's flower shop as a teenager, where her experience with flowering plants and eye for design grew. After leaving school, she worked for an independent lifestyle store, which ignited her love of homewares, interiors and visual merchandising. During this time, she started a small company with a friend and colleague, and together they developed a more well-rounded view of business. In 2012, she returned to The Fresh Flower Company where, having continuously studied the growth habits of indoor plants, she and her mum Fran introduced a selection of houseplants to their customers. The decision to open Forest, a houseplant and lifestyle store, came shortly afterwards, as the popularity around indoor plants heightened. With their combined love of business and shared knowledge of the plant industry, they, together with Maddie, evolved the business into what it is today.

THE HIDDEN HISTORIES *of* HOUSE PLANTS

Fascinating stories
of our most-loved
houseplants

Maddie & Alice Bailey

Hardie Grant

BOOKS

Introduction

While they have become increasingly popular over the past decade or so, the idea of houseplants isn't particularly new; in fact, they've been cultivated over a century. A great number of us living all around the world have been drawn in by the trend and the concept of having greenery indoors, and as we learn more about how to keep houseplants at home, we find ourselves becoming more curious about the lives they lead in the wild. The plants we call 'houseplants' in much of Western society aren't necessarily houseplants everywhere – cult classics like the infamous spider plant or the towering, cheese-like monstera grew up in very different conditions to the conditions we keep them in at home.

Many of us buy houseplants to remind ourselves of all the beauty the natural world has to offer, from large-leaved variegated plants from the depths of the jungles in South East Asia to twisted and unusual succulents in the deserts of South Africa; houseplants give us a glimpse of exotic plant life that is often unobtainable. Our homes can become protective greenhouses which allow plant life to thrive and flourish – and yet many of us don't recognise the incredible feats of engineering through centuries of evolution that give our houseplants their most striking and unusual appearances.

Have you ever wondered, for example, why there are holes in the leaves of your monstera plant? And what's the deal with aloe vera?

Does it puzzle you that calathea leaves open during the day and close up at night? In the comfort of our homes, the reasons why might not be so obvious, but the countless adaptations, unusual habits, movements and colours serve very real purposes in the wild. Observing these behaviours over years surrounded by houseplants and the growing trend made us eager to learn more about plant intelligence, how they function in the natural world and in diverse cultures, and how these humble plants have evolved to adapt to unfavourable conditions. We compiled a list of 20 different houseplants that display unique and unusual behaviours, and studied and researched each one until we found answers to some of our most burning houseplant questions. Along the way, we found our questions changing and evolving, and so the book has evolved with us – and we have included all our most interesting findings here. At the start of each profile, we have included a map of the main native locations.

If, like us, you find yourself ever more curious, beyond the aesthetic of a home filled with plants, and yearn to know more about the inner workings of your houseplant companions, then join us on our journey to discover how they came to be the plants we all know and love today.

CHAPTER 1

LEAVES

Monstera Deliciosa

(cheese or Swiss cheese plant)

Native Location
Mexico

Monstera deliciosa, AKA the cheese or Swiss cheese plant, is probably the most well-known houseplant to have graced the market in the last 50 years. They're a staple for indoor cultivation since you can buy them pretty much anywhere and they aren't too challenging to grow. The nickname 'cheese plant' refers to the renowned holes in their leaves (known botanically as 'leaf fenestration'); this unusual appearance is what has made them so popular as a houseplant.

Throughout the 1960s and early 1970s, monstera were arguably one of the most popular houseplants (followed closely by spider plants, palms and Boston ferns) and were grown by everyone, houseplant connoisseur or not. At the very least, most people owned an item of clothing, piece of furniture or décor with a monstera-leaf print.

By the 1980s, however, minimalism had taken off, and many houseplants were cast out to the compost heap. Because of this, monstera (and a few others, like the humble spider plant) can be purchased, for many, with a free flashback to the 1970s – something those who lived through the first wave of houseplant mania might be reluctant to relive.

For those born after the initial craze, monstera have become a firm favourite once more and can often be found nestled among alocasia and other interesting tropical species in modern interior magazines and books, this time bringing forth an image of a lush,

dark green tropical forest – a slice of jungle in a concrete city.

Their famous hole-ridden leaves have been printed onto notebooks, wallpaper, bedding, clothes, cushions and pretty much any other interior fabric you can think of – people wear monstera-shaped earrings and get monstera-leaf tattoos, so it's no surprise that most of us, whether new to or well acquainted with the houseplant craze, have them growing at home.

Aside from their instantly recognisable leaves, there is another attribute which draws people to cheese plants: their name. After all, *Monstera deliciosa* is intriguing and gives off an air of mystery – and you don't have to be able to speak Latin to understand it. Monstera derives from the Latin *monstrum*, meaning 'monster', and refers to the plant's monstrous size. In the wild, monstera can grow to be over 9 metres (30 feet) tall, with leaves as big as 1 metres (3 feet) wide, although in cultivation, monstera rarely grow to be taller than 3 metres (10 feet), making them less monstera and more 'averagea'.

Deliciosa translates to 'delicious', and the reason monstera have been awarded this species name is because of the delicious and rare fruit they produce – a delicacy in the countries they come from. Unfortunately, it's near impossible to encourage a cultivated monstera to fruit outside of its natural habitat, the conditions of which are rarely met in our homes.

A WALK ON THE WILD SIDE

Monstera grow naturally in pretty much any region with a tropical or sub-tropical climate: countries such as Costa Rica, Brazil, Mexico, Indonesia and China provide the perfect climate for them to thrive. They are usually found in rainforests and other plant biomes but can be found growing up a tree or structure in any shaded, humid spot. They aren't too fussy about their surroundings as long as they are provided adequate food, water and space to climb and grow.

Monstera are hemiepiphytic vines, which means they grow in the ground initially, and once they reach a supporting structure, such as a tree, they produce support roots along their stems to help to stabilise them on the structure as they climb. They also produce fast-growing aerial roots that dangle down beside them and reach into the soil, providing the plant with the nutrients and water necessary to survive.

In rainforests, young seedlings grow along the ground towards the darkest spot – this action is known as negative phototropism (positive phototropism is when a plant grows towards the nearest light source). The seedlings do this to find the shadow of a supporting object like a tree, which they can climb. Once they have found a tree, they begin their ascent, this time using positive phototropism to climb up as quickly as possible towards the light from the canopy layer of the rainforest.

HOLES IN THE THEORIES

The monstera has gained a lot of its popularity from the unique holes in its leaves. But why exactly does it produce these holes? One could assume the leaves were cultivated that way on purpose, but they weren't. The holes do serve a purpose in the wild.

Since the leaves of any plant serve the purpose of harvesting light, it stands to reason that they produce the holes to gain some kind of advantage in the low light situations they grow in. It's hard to pinpoint the exact reason the plant does it, but here are a few theories:

To protect itself in a storm: for the same reason banana plants (musa) and birds of paradise (strelitzia) produce slits in the sides of their leaves: to allow wind to pass through during hurricanes and strong winds. Plants that grow tall run into problems if they have big leaves – without protection from surrounding plants and structures, they're left exposed. And the bigger their leaves are, the more likely they are to be damaged or torn in stormy conditions, which are common during the rainy season in tropical climates. While this theory makes a lot of sense for banana plants, monstera are very rarely found growing in exposed conditions where they would be strongly affected by wind, so this theory doesn't have a lot of backbone.

To regulate its temperature: Plants growing in the rainforest understory (the layer closest to the ground) are able to survive with large leaves because the temperature drops the closer to the forest floor you get. The theory suggests that monstera, which grow closer to the canopy layer than other large-leaved plants, struggle to regulate their temperature and so produce holes to allow for more air movement through the leaf.

To camouflage itself: The downside to this theory is that it doesn't explain why younger leaves don't produce holes. Younger leaves would benefit the most from camouflage as they are closest to the ground and still at risk of encountering herbivores – yet only the light-exposed monstera leaves, which are further up the plant, produce holes.

SOAKING UP THE SUN

Our theory, which is supported by some other plant experts, is that the leaves at the top of the vine, which have made the climb to the brightest light, develop holes to allow light through to the leaves growing beneath them. And their natural habitat seems to support this thinking.

In the canopy layer of the rainforest, most available light comes in the form of sun flecks – small, concentrated pools of unobscured light which filter through the canopy. They're like energy-rich nutrient bars to a monstera. Depending on the density of the canopy above, these sun flecks can be few and far between, which means the monstera needs large leaves to increase its chance of catching them.

Rather than waste energy producing huge, full leaves, the theory suggests that monstera creates holes in its leaves, allowing for a larger surface area without expending as much energy while also increasing its chance of catching sun flecks. A number of studies found that leaves with the same surface area, but without the holes, absorb less sunlight than monstera leaves.

This also explains why younger leaves don't produce as many, if any, holes. As explained earlier, young seedlings grow towards the shadiest part of the forest to find a tree to climb, but actually the majority of the understory layer of the rainforest is in deep shade. The further up the canopy you go, the more available light there is, so younger leaves and seedlings don't produce holes because it simply isn't necessary, there isn't enough light to warrant doing so.

This theory also helps with regards to cultivating monstera at home. Many people want to know why their monstera leaves aren't producing holes, and the reason is simple: because they aren't getting enough light.

FRUITS OF THEIR LABOUR

As previously discussed, the *deliciosa* species name stems from the delicious fruit the plant produces. Monstera are a part of the Araceae family, which includes plants like peace lilies, anthuriums, arums and many others. Characteristic of any plant family are their flowers. Flowers from the Araceae family are borne on a spadix, surrounded by a protective bract called a spathe (think of the flowers on a peace lily). The spathe dies and falls away after the flowers have been pollinated, and the central spadix begins to grow into fruit.

The fruit itself – known as ceriman or Mexican breadfruit – can take years to ripen, and if eaten unripe can make your mouth and oesophagus burn because of a chemical called oxalic acid. One use for concentrated oxalic acid is rust removal, so you can imagine why it's not ideal to consume in large quantities. The amount of oxalic acid in the fruit drops drastically to a level found in many other fruits and vegetables once it ripens, making it safe to eat.

As the fruit slowly matures, it starts to resemble corn on the cob (but much bigger), and before it becomes fully ripe, the hexagonal scales which cover the fruit grow larger and begin to protrude, turning from green to yellow, similarly to a banana. While this process is happening, the fruit emits a delicious, sweet scent, which grows stronger as the fruit matures. When the scales turn fully yellow and start dropping off, the fruit is ready to eat. When fully ripe, it's about the size of a large courgette and the scent disappears. There's only a short window to eat the fruit before it goes bad.

We've never tried it, but, according to those who have, it is exquisite and tastes like a combination between a banana and a pineapple, with a similar texture to the latter. Monstera fruit are a delicacy and are hard to come by if you live outside a country where they are found growing naturally.

A HOUSEPLANT STAPLE

Whatever the image of a *Monstera deliciosa* leaf conjures up for you, whether it be a cringe-inducing flashback or the image of a tropical rainforest – it's undeniable that monstera have been at the forefront of houseplant cultivation for a very long time and for good reason.

Although new, and arguably more exciting, plants with exotic and unusual leaves are being cultivated by houseplant growers all the time, the true beauty of the monstera is reflected in its own adaptation – it made the leaves that way by itself. And for whatever reason, its leaves are truly a work of art.

"The forest is for me a temple – a cathedral of tree canopies and dancing light."

—

Dr Jane Goodall,
primatologist

Begonia

Native Locations
Central and
South America,
South East Asia,
Sub-Saharan Africa

Begonia is a genus of flowering plants within its own family (Begoniaceae), and they are beloved by expert and amateur alike. The plants have always been popular for their striking and unusual foliage and delicate flowers, and are cultivated by many as both a houseplant and a garden plant, depending on the species. Most species within the *Begonia* genus can be found growing in tropical and subtropical regions, but since they are part of such a large and popular family, they are cultivated in different climes across the globe.

WHAT'S IN A NAME?

As a result of global cultivation, begonia nomenclature (naming) can be extremely complex – species within the genus are easily bred both in cultivation and in nature, creating a long line of varieties, cultivars and hybrids, which can be difficult to trace.

Before we venture too much further into the world of begonia naming, it may help to clarify the differences between 'variety', 'cultivar' and 'hybrid' first. If two plants of the same species produce offspring with a few characteristic differences to their parent plants, the offspring is known either as a variety or a cultivar. A variety occurs in the wild, without human intervention, while a cultivar

is man-made (or made in cultivation). The word 'cultivar' itself is a combination of the words 'cultivated' and 'variety'. Finally, a hybrid is a plant produced either naturally or in cultivation and is the offspring of two *different* species in the same genus, often displaying characteristics of both parent plants. All three terms refer to a deviation from the parent species, which is why tracing the origin of many begonias, especially those resulting from already hybridised plants, can be extremely difficult.

In an attempt to make things a little easier, members of the American Begonia Society have unofficially grouped begonias based on visual attributes and growth habits. They categorise the plants as follows: cane-like (with thick stems that loosely resemble bamboo), shrub-like (forming a shrub growth habit), tuberous (referring to tuberous roots), rhizomatous (a type of modified root), semperflorens (a well-known species commonly grown for its flowers), 'Rex' (a diverse cultivar commonly grown for its leaves), trailing-scandent (vine-like) and, finally, thick-stemmed begonias, which produce tree-trunk like stems. This grouping system is not official, nor is it scientific, but it is used by many (including the Royal Horticultural Society), and does help to organise the multitude of begonias both on the market and in the wild.

NATURE VS NURTURE

To many, the most attracting feature of a begonia is its leaves (although many are grown for their flowers), which display a great number of patterns, colours and variegations, occurring both in cultivation and in nature. Many of the cultivars we buy have been bred to display an array of striking and unusual patterns, and they have long been the subject of intrigue in plant displays throughout the horticultural world.

While man-made cultivars are certainly popular, perhaps some of the most visually striking aspects of begonias are the result of naturally occurring varieties harvested by man and bred to create interesting new cultivars. Many of these sought-after, wild varieties have evolved over long periods of time as a result of a life lived in unfavourable conditions, or as a way to increase success in the wild while expending minimal effort and energy. These adaptations, far from simply being nice to look at, serve a very real purpose in the wild, and are a wonderful example of how quietly complex nature can be.

THE GOLDEN SPIRAL

Aside from their attractive colour and interesting variegations, the leaves of many begonia species boast another interest: their shape. Cultivars such as *Begonia* 'Escargot' have foliage which grows in a beautifully precise spiral formation, like the shell of a sea creature or a snail, which is where the 'Escargot' cultivar name comes from. While this striking leaf formation is perhaps the most noticeable in the 'Escargot' cultivar, many other species of begonia display the very same spiral formation. The more commonly grown *Begonia* 'Rex' cultivar is another wonderful example. But it's not just in the leaves of a begonia that this pattern emerges. It can be found in almost every aspect of nature – from the seeds of a sunflower, to the whirling formation of the leaves on an echeveria, and countless other succulent plants. If you take the time to observe the natural world, you will see it everywhere.

In mathematics, the number pattern reflected in this spiral shape is known as the Fibonacci sequence. The sequence itself is easy enough to understand. It's a series where each number is the sum of the previous two; the simplest being: 0, 1, 1, 2, 3, 5, 8, 13, 21, 34, 55, 89 and so on. These numbers go on infinitely and, in their prime form, the Fibonacci spiral, which is the mathematical basis for almost all of the natural world. It is often visualised as a seashell-shaped spiral, beginning small and gradually increasing.

The spiral leaves of numerous species of begonia display the sequence perfectly, and it can be immensely satisfying to the eye. It's extremely useful to the leaves, because it allows for the most efficient growth to take place; the leaves grow at a constantly increasing size, without any change in shape, making this spiralling a

"The Fibonacci numbers … appear everywhere in nature, from the leaf arrangement in plants, to the pattern of florets in a flower, the bracts of a pine cone, or the scales of a pineapple. The Fibonacci numbers are therefore applicable to the growth of every living thing, including a single cell, a grain of wheat, a hive of bees and even all of mankind."

—

Nikhat Parveen, Biochemist,
University of Georgia

near-perfect pattern (environmental factors allowing). But it is not just the leaf growth on a begonia that follows the Fibonacci spiral. The leaf arrangement on the stem (known as leaf phyllotaxy) follows this growth progression as well. By growing its leaves in a Fibonacci sequence around the stem, the plant maximises the sun uptake of each leaf as it's maturing, making sure that the growth of one leaf doesn't hinder the photosynthetic process of another. This arrangement also means that rainwater is more able to reach the soil below the plant and doesn't get stuck in a succession of tightly packed leaves.

There are hundreds of thousands of plants in nature that produce this satisfying spiral formation, whether it be in leaf phyllotaxis, the growth and production of stems, or in the leaves themselves. It has been observed in animals, fungi and all other aspects of nature, as well as in architecture and art, from the Renaissance to modern abstract art and photography, and even in music. The Fibonacci sequence has been used in algorithms and patterns in economics and trading, numerous sciences, and in countless other fields which impact our lives on a day-to-day basis.

IRIDESCENT BEGONIA

As we are well aware by now, *Begonia* is a diverse, beautiful and colourful genus. But as houseplant lovers, one species in particular stands out to us among the rest: *B. pavonina*, aptly nicknamed the 'peacock begonia'. This particular species is endemic to Malaysia, where it can be found in the rainforest understory, growing in deep shade. Due to the difficulties it faces growing in such an unfavourable habitat, *B. pavonina* has developed a rather unique set of characteristics. It has iridescent, sparkling blue leaves, which, although they look as though they've been cultivated by man, occur naturally. This iridescence is an evolutionary adaptation shared with various other species growing in the deep shade of the understory. It allows the begonia to efficiently absorb light waves that other plants might not be able to.

Rather than having chloroplasts (parts of cells which absorb light for photosynthesis), the peacock begonia has a different type of organelle – dubbed an 'iridoplast'. These iridoplasts serve the same purpose as chlorophyll but are much better at absorbing light in deep shade. They have a unique composition within the leaf, one which is not seen in plants that produce chlorophyll; the iridoplasts are stacked on top of each other, with a thin layer of liquid between them. This bends the light that passes through the leaf, causing a reflected shimmer known as 'interference'. This is the same kind of rainbow shimmer we might see on the road when oil from an engine ends up in a puddle.

In the understory, the canopy and its bright light are far away. Visible light is measured on a spectrum, with wavelengths that match colour. Some wavelengths are short and therefore more powerful, while other wavelengths are long and gentle. But not all of them are powerful enough to reach the understory layer of the rainforest. Most comes in the form of long, gentle green wavelengths, and iridoplasts have a much easier time harvesting this light than chloroplasts do. Blue wavelengths are also able to penetrate down into the depths of the understory, but these, by contrast, are short and harsh, and could easily damage the iridoplasts of the delicate begonia. As a result, the begonia absorbs the 'safer' green wavelength, while reflecting the 'harsh' blue wavelength. And it's this reflection that causes the leaves of a peacock begonia to appear blue instead of green.

This special plant looks perfectly at home in the mystical depths of tropical rainforests, where the image of glowing toadstools and luminous frogs can easily be conjured up. Its fascinating composition has sparked a great deal of interest among houseplant lovers and plant growers alike.

A GORGEOUS, GRACEFUL GRANNY

While iridescence and the Fibonacci spiral are by no means unique to the leaves of a begonia, these nature-borne adaptations stand out in this particular genus of plants, especially when you take their long and untraceable lineage of cultivars, hybrids and varieties into consideration. The appearance of many common begonias has been changed, and then changed again, until all unique characteristics are uncertain and cultivars no longer stand apart from natural varieties; though perhaps this is all part of the appeal. Much like they did in the Dutch tulip craze, interesting cultivars become collectibles, with social media and houseplant influencers boosting the mania.

While some still view the more 'traditional' varieties and cultivars of begonia as 'granny plants', it's safe to say that the plants are coming back in full force. So we can all expect to keep enjoying the interesting and vast varieties available to us from country to country for years to come.

Calathea

Native Locations
The Amazon
Rainforest in Brazil,
Colombia and Bolivia

"Nothing could be more striking than the rapid change by which a patch of vivid green becomes transformed into thin lines of dull green unnoticed against the dark ground. The plant thus saves itself by literally 'lying low' and becoming invisible."

—— Sir Jagadish Chandra Bose, biologist

Calathea is a genus of tropical plants that has gained massive popularity as part of the houseplant trend. These plants are renowned for their extremely decorative foliage, and the multitude of cultivars that are available on the market. It seems with every month that passes, exciting new cultivars become available, spurring on a whole new lease of excitement in the world of exotic-plant collectors.

The plants themselves can be difficult to keep – this is mostly because recreating the conditions they find the most favourable in our homes is challenging, and care requirements vary depending on where they are located in your home. But once the right conditions are found, they are a sight to behold. They are not only satisfying to look at, but also help to instil some houseplant-y confidence in their owners.

As with all other houseplants we grow, understanding a calathea's native climate and the behaviours the plant exhibits is key to solving the puzzle of how to keep them happy and healthy at home.

CHAPTER 1: LEAVES 25

RAINFOREST BIOME

Calathea are native to the rainforests of the tropical Americas in places like Brazil, Paraguay, Venezuela and Ecuador, among many others.

In the rainforest, there are distinct layers of vegetation. The canopy layer, where the trees create a tall umbrella over the biome below, is the brightest, being the closest to the light. The canopy layer is usually 35–40 metres (114–131 feet) up from ground level. The further down you go, the dimmer the light becomes. Past the understory, there is the forest floor, which sits in deep shade. This is where calathea and other shade-tolerant plants can be found growing.

Because of the protection provided by the trees and larger plants, there is very little air movement, and so this layer is also extremely humid. A relatively cool temperature and no extreme dips or rises throughout the seasons is characteristic of a tropical climate, and so calathea grow in balmy, humid warmth year-round. Because of the high humidity, the soil never dries out too much, and the plants lose minimal water to the warm atmosphere.

Many characteristics of a calathea, whether they are found in cultivation or not, are a testament to their natural habitat. Their leaves tend to grow large, while being delicate and papery. This helps them to harvest as much natural light as possible in their shady dwellings, without wasting energy producing unnecessarily thick leaves (since they don't need protection from any drying winds or hot sun).

The typically purple colouring on the underside or full leaf of a calathea also has a purpose in the wild. As we discuss in our sections on echeveria (page 114) and begonia (page 16), purple leaves indicate a higher level of the pigment 'anthocyanin'. Anthocyanin helps plants to absorb green light, whose wavelengths are long and gentle, and more able to reach the forest floor. This means that the leaves of a calathea have a much easier time absorbing light when more of the anthocyanin pigment is present; the leaves appear to us as purple, blue or red. It is also thought that higher levels of anthocyanin in a plant go hand in hand with higher levels of poisonous phenols (organic compounds) – and so plants with purple leaves are much less likely to be attacked by hungry herbivores, who fear the 'purple poison'.

LEAF MOVEMENT

As well as their more visible adaptations, there is another adaptation which stands out to many, and also helps the plant to survive in low light levels: the movement of their leaves.

This adaptation is fairly straightforward and occurs in quite a few species of shade-tolerant plants, such as *Maranta sp.*, which is a member of the same family as a calathea, Marantaceae. This movement of leaves occurs when the light levels change or, more specifically, when day turns to night – and is known botanically as nyctinasty. This movement of the leaves once the sun has gone down has long been a subject of curiosity for botanists and biologists. We also discuss this phenomenon in the section on night flowers (page 46).

During the day, plants which have foliar nyctinasty have their leaves laid horizontally, as most other terrestrial (ground-dwelling) plant species do, allowing them to harvest sunlight. As the sun begins to set and darkness falls over the rainforest (or the rooms in our home), the leaves slowly begin to move, using specialised hinges at the end of their petiole (leaf stalk), until their leaf tips are facing the sky in a vertical position.

Foliar nyctinasty was first recorded by Androsthenes, an admiral of Alexander the Great, back in 324 BCE. And it has been observed in the leaves and flowers of many different species ever since. Carl Linnaeus, the Swedish botanist who came up with the idea of nomenclature, suggested in 1759 that the leaves of nyctinastic plants close at night to 'sleep'. But this idea was, and still is, widely disregarded, as plants would need to be proven to be conscious beings in order to have the ability to experience the altered consciousness of sleep.

THEORIES BEHIND THE MOVEMENT

So what causes this phenomenon? Why do the leaves of some plants close at night? While there are many theories, none have yet been proven. Foliar nyctinasty is still a bit of a mystery, despite the phenomenon having been observed and studied for over two millennia. There are, however, a number of plausible theories, which could help explain this unusual behaviour.

Charles Darwin suggested that the closing up of a plant's leaves was a way for the plant to regulate its temperature and avoid being badly affected by colder evenings or even frosts. He surmised that by raising their leaves, the leaf blade (either side of the central vein) was not directly exposed to cold night-time air from above, and that the leaf blades would expose their undersides to warmer objects nearby, such as stones or other plants. While this theory is plausible, it doesn't account for plants living in tropical or subtropical climates, where night-time temperatures rarely drop and plants are sheltered from any cooler air by larger plants and trees.

Another theory suggests that nyctinastic plants close their leaves at night to rid themselves of any water that has collected on their leaves during the day and/or to avoid the build-up of night-time dew. Research and study on this hypothesis suggests that nyctinastic plants are able to shed dew and captured water much more quickly than plants with leaves that remain horizontal throughout the night – but the question remains: is it really necessary? The movement of leaves from horizontal to vertical is an energy-consuming one for any plant. And for calathea, there really isn't much to be gained from it – having dew or a bit of water on its leaves will do the plant no harm. Surely it would be a waste of energy to perform such an arduous task every day only to remove a small amount of water from its leaves?

One theory, which seems to make the most sense, suggests that plants practise foliar nyctinasty as a way to protect themselves from nocturnal herbivores. The theory suggests that when plants close their leaves upwards, taking a bite, or indeed, even getting a grip on the leaves becomes much more difficult for whatever might want to eat them. This certainly makes a lot of sense in the case of a calathea, especially when you consider that many species' leaves have purple undersides, making them extremely well camouflaged against the seeking eyes of a herbivore in the darkness of night. Perhaps the smartest part of the theory is the idea that by having their leaves up, nyctinastic plants create less ground cover for these herbivores. The herbivores are then much more visible to their own predators.

This theory also explains why foliar nyctinasty occurs in many different species of plants living in varying climates across the globe – all could fall prey to hungry herbivores, no matter their native habitat. And they need all the help they can ge,t because the high levels of nitrogen found in the foliage of many species makes them an attractive meal – nitrogen is an essential nutrient for any herbivore. While intelligent and undoubtedly plausible, the theory hasn't yet been scientifically proven.

Whatever the reason for this unusual phenomenon, it is interesting to observe, and perhaps now when your calathea or maranta closes its leaves for the night, you'll have a new-found fascination for the plant.

CHAPTER 2

FLOWERS

Stapelia

(carrion flower)

Native Location
South Africa

Stapelia is a relatively small genus of succulents that, at first glance, are unremarkable. There are only around 50 different species within the genus, all of which can be found growing in South Africa. Every species looks pretty similar, with a few exceptions (their habit of growth is really the defining feature between species). Their succulent (water-storing) stems grow upright and could almost resemble some kind of aquatic plant, or a euphorbia (page 54), until gravity does its job, and their stems end up trailing or crawling.

Stapelia, commonly called carrion flower, do technically produce leaves, but they're tiny and a bit useless – often drying up and dying before they have the chance to fully develop. As with many other succulents, stapelia instead rely on their all-purpose stems to photosynthesise, as well as to store water for periods of drought. Although these plants might not look like much to begin with, their simple form is a guise for something much more spectacular.

STINKY STAPELIA SURPRISE

The stapelia first presented itself to us as a bundle of ordinary-looking stems (which we presumed belonged to the *Euphorbia* genus). Over time, we noticed a flower bud forming – and considering

the stems were no longer than 10 cm (4 in) each, the buds were enormous! As soon as it flowered, we learned where the true beauty of a stapelia lies.

The starfish-shaped flowers are magnificent, other-worldly and undeniably unique. They can take on a great number of different textures, colours and sizes. Some are soft and furry, while others are ridged and rubbery. They can be yellow, red, purple, peach or a combination of colours. They also smell absolutely revolting.

Mimicking the scent of rotting flesh, hence the name 'carrion', stapelia definitely have their pollinators in mind when producing their characteristic stink. The scent the flowers produce attracts necrophagous insects (insects that feed off decaying tissue) such as blowflies, flesh flies, houseflies and some beetles. The insects mistake the scent for a dead animal, then go on to lay eggs, or mate, pollinating the flowers in the process.

THE SCIENCE BEHIND THE SMELL

There are various compounds responsible for producing the revolting stench of stapelia flowers and other sapromyiophilous flowers – flowers that attract flies and insects by mimicking the scent of carrion. They include trimethylamine, which is responsible for the odour of rotting fish, and isocaproic acid, which creates the smell of cheesy feet. Stapelia flowers also give off a scent of dung – the result of a few different compounds working together. The main scent, though, comes from oligosulphides, which are the compounds responsible for the scent of rotting flesh.

How have these plants evolved over time to realise that the scent which attracts its pollinators is rotting flesh? We imagine it was a survival-of-the-fittest type response. It's possible stapelia with high levels of the stinky compounds were pollinated more than those without, encouraging a much more pungent odour through the generations. Although unpleasant for us, it's absolutely incredible to think that plants are capable of understanding their pollinators in enough depth to trick the insects for their own benefit.

"Scent is a powerful lure. We are familiar with the lush exotics and delicate florals, but mother nature is no prude. The carrion flowers, also known as corpse flowers, are a whole group of flowering plants that choose to go the darker side of the olfactive spectrum."

—

Nuri McBride,
Founder of the Death/Scent project,
in the essay "The Carrion Flowers"

Orchids

Native Locations
Tropical Asia, tropical
Australia and tropical
South America

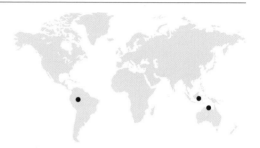

"In my examination of Orchids, hardly any fact has so much struck me as the endless diversity of structure ... for gaining the very same end, namely, the fertilisation of one flower by the pollen of another."

—— **Charles Darwin,** naturalist
On the various contrivances by
which British and foreign orchids
are fertilised by insects

Orchids are the second largest family of flowering plants in the world. With over 750 genera and more than 25,000 accepted species, it's no surprise they're so popular. Because the family is so diverse, they can be found growing anywhere on Earth, even in the Arctic Circle; in fact, the only habitat where you can't find orchids growing naturally is on glaciers.

An exhumed fossil, dated between 15 to 20 million years ago, featured an extinct species of bee trapped in amber with orchid pollen on its wings. This proves that orchids are one of the oldest families of flowering plants too; and with all that time on their hands, they've done some pretty spectacular evolving.

Of course, the most impressive aspect of an orchid is its flowers – which are the reason most of us buy them in supermarkets, florists and houseplant shops. Since orchids only flower five to seven years

after germination, most of the orchids bought on the market are already a decade old.

When it comes to successfully keeping orchids alive, it seems some struggle more than others. The truth is, it can be hard to find out how to grow your orchid simply because the family is so diverse – there's no one-size-fits-all guide to growing them. If your orchid is naturally terrestrial and comes from Europe, it will require very different care to an epiphytic orchid naturally found growing in Borneo.

This is the same reason some types of orchid are more readily available than others – and we are seldom exposed to rare and 'difficult' orchid breeds, which only specialists seem able to cultivate. This makes them all the more enticing and attractive when seen in horticultural displays, in exotic-plant nurseries or at specialist stands at plant fairs.

LURING POLLINATORS IN

But it is not just people who are lured by the impressive and seem-ingly limitless array of different orchids flowers. They produce these flowers for one reason alone: to attract pollinators. Each different type of orchid has developed the most effective way of luring its pollinators over time, and the expanse of unique and compelling flowers reflects this. No plant would develop such unique flowers without purpose.

Although orchid flowers very rarely reward their pollinators with nectar, these plants have developed a multitude of different ways to fool their pollinators into thinking otherwise. Some orchids pepper their petals with colourful blotches to mimic the anthers and pollen sacs of other flowers that produce an abundance of nectar, while others use 'sexual deception' to lure their pollinators in. Some orchids produce scent and others enchant with bright, luminous colours.

As far as successful pollination goes, it has been proven that orchid species that have adapted with one sole pollinator in mind are more likely to achieve successful pollination than those pollinated by multiple species; as with many things in life, those who have worked harder achieve the most success.

There are a great number of complex pollinator-focused mechanisms orchids or, more specifically, orchid flowers use to achieve the best results. Here are some of the most interesting adaptations found in the most common household orchids.

MASTERS OF SEXUAL DECEPTION

Ophrys, or 'bee orchids', are a very interesting orchid genus. Members of the genus are known to be masters of deception. They can be found growing in Europe and North Africa, but are mostly found in the Mediterranean.

Each individual species has adapted its flowers to suit its own particular pollinator – *Ophrys bombyliflora*, for example, attracts bumblebees. Meanwhile, *Ophrys lutea* attract yellow bees, and a quick google will show you why. The shape of the flower itself says a lot about the way these plants are pollinated.

Ophrys species' incredible adaptation is that their flowers perfectly resemble their pollinators, specifically the female of the pollinators they're trying to attract. Usually this is a bee or wasp. Even more incredibly, a number of species within the genus are also able to recreate the pheromones secreted by the female pollinator through their flowers. This is known as sexual deception.

A male pollinator first smells the pheromones, which play the most important part in attracting a mate and then, upon spotting the flower (which looks almost identical to the female), flies over to mate. During the mating attempt, known as pseudocopulation, the pollinator brushes against the pollinium (a mass of pollen grains), which attach to his body. Once he has done the deed, he flies off, noticing yet another 'willing female' to mate with. In his attempt to copulate again, he brushes the pollen collected from the previous flower onto the stigma (female sex organ) of the next.

Sometimes the pheromones produced by the flower are so strong that the male pollinator will choose to mate with the flower instead of a true female.

THE EUGLOSSINE BEE'S
EXHAUSTING ENDEAVOUR

Coryanthes, also known as bucket orchids, use a luring and trapping mechanism to achieve successful pollination. They too, had one particular species in mind when evolving their flowers: the euglossine bee. In fact, the two evolved together, forming a mutually beneficial relationship.

Coryanthes species' flowers are the heaviest among orchids, with a modified labellum (the pollinator-attracting lip of the flower) turned into a bucket-shaped pitfall (like a shallow pitcher plant), which hangs below the other parts of the flower. In total, the flowers can weigh up to 100 g (3½ oz) each. This bucket contains perfumed, oily secretions which the neon green euglossine bees covet above all else.

Catching scent of the oily secretions, the bee flies over to collect some. The pitcher itself is extremely slippery so any attempt to stay on the side or on the lip that sits above the bucket is futile. He inevitably falls into the oil and is coated from head to toe. He can't fly off because his wings are covered in oil, and he can't climb out because the walls are too slippery.

But there is one positive to this experience, and that is the very thing that landed him in this predicament in the first place: the oily secretions. Male euglossine bees use the oil to attract females, and without it, their chances of mating would diminish. So he loads up special sacs on his back legs with the oil and plans his escape.

There is only one way out, and that is through a small opening in the back wall of the bucket. Gripping on for dear life, he climbs the wall and crawls through the opening, which sits just below where the pollen and the stigma are held. As he squeezes past, the pollinium attaches itself onto his head or back. Then, after a bit of a rest on the back of the flower, he is finally free to go. In total, this ordeal can take up to 45 minutes, and is exhausting for the bee. So you may ask, why does he bother? Well, aside from the necessity of collecting the oils for his mating ritual, the truth is he forgets. Not long after he flies away, he's lured once again by another *Coryanthes* orchid –

whereupon he deposits the pollen onto the stigma of the next flower and completes the pollination cycle.

The oils secreted have been made with only the euglossine bee in mind, and the transaction benefits both parties equally, allowing both to reproduce and continue their genetic line. Larger bees would fall into the trap and, unable to climb through the small opening at the back, die. Smaller bees would be able to climb through the back, but not pollinate the orchid. Interestingly, this agreement is also extremely useful to hazelnut production, since hazelnut plants also rely on euglossine bees for pollination – and euglossine bees could not survive without *Coryanthes* orchids.

This orchid, however, is not easy to grow, and is among the least common genera found as a houseplant. Although they are difficult to cultivate, it is getting much easier to keep them indoors, and specialists grow them with a lot of love and appreciation.

PERFECTLY ENGINEERED POLLEN ATTACK

The *Catasetum* orchid genus deserves a special spot on the list. Not least because it is so beloved to orchid specialists and plant cultivators, but it was also Darwin's favourite. After studying their innovative adaptation for years, he coined *Catasetum* 'the most remarkable of all orchids', surely a high enough compliment to inspire exploration of their inner workings.

As with many other of Darwin's favourite plant subjects, *Catasetum* have a complex and unusual way of working around everyday situations; they don't deceive their pollinators as many other orchids do. Instead, male flowers expel their pollen at pollinators at high speed.

Not all *Catasetum* are the same – male and female flowers in this genus differ massively. Male flowers are brightly coloured and open, while female flowers are dull green in colour and grow a 'hood' over their flower parts. This distinct variation between male and female flowers is known in the natural world as sexual dimorphism and is very rarely seen in the orchid family, making this genus even more remarkable.

Even more interestingly, both male and female flowers can be found blooming on the same plant at the same time, confusing plant taxonomists, who previously thought the flowers must have belonged to separate species. Some *Catasetum* can even grow female flowers, male flowers, and hermaphrodite flowers all on the same plant – and each flower looks totally different.

The sex of the flower itself is often determined by available light: flowers growing in brighter sunlight are usually female, while those growing in shadier positions are usually male. And just to add a little more confusion into the mix, it is possible for male flowers to turn into female flowers if exposed to brighter light, and vice versa.

The real kicker here, though, is that the unfortunate pollinator subject to exhausting trials with the *Coryanthes* orchid (and its oily bucket) is the very same pollinator on the receiving end of the this genus' pollen shotgun: the poor euglossine bee.

Euglossine bees mate for life, and so the males must do everything they possibly can to attract the attention of a female, including collecting the scented oils mentioned earlier to make themselves more attractive. Male *Catasetum* orchids first lure the bee by releasing an early-morning scent. It is vital that the male flower is able to lure the bee in before the female flower (if he went to the female first, the ritual would not work). Upon arriving at the male flower, the bee walks around to collect the oils. The flower contains a kind of sterile, false stigma (female sex organ) in the middle, from which a pair of small antennae protrude. When the antennae are triggered by the bee, the *Catasetum* shoots out a two-part projectile of viscidium (a sort of sticky arrowhead) and pollinium, which fixes onto the bee.

This pollen attack is understandably very startling to the bee (who is only twice the size of the pollinium). He's expelled with such force (the same force as the striking head of a pit-viper) that it has been known, on occasion, to knock the bees out for a short time. Because of this forceful and surprising strike, the bee is understandably resentful, and unlikely to return to the male flower head until he forgets the ordeal. He will instead visit the female flower (which looks totally different, and much friendlier than the flower he's just encountered) to complete the pollination cycle.

Although arduous for the euglossine bee, this process is extremely successful for the *Catasetum*, with every pollinator that leaves the orchid fertilising the next.

ONCIDIUM AND THE ANGRY SWARM

A genus also known as the dancing-lady orchid, is one of the most well-known and perhaps one of the easiest to keep. But outside of our households, *Oncidium* live in a different world – one in which they are master tricksters, and have developed their own unique survival regiment.

The flowers produced by *Oncidium* orchids (specifically *Oncidium orquidea*) are small, but large in number. The petiole which attaches the flower head to the main stem is thin and allows the flowers to dance around in the breeze, awarding them their common name. This 'dancing' is certainly meant to attract pollinators; however, one theory suggests that this behaviour is not meant to beguile them but actually the opposite – it is meant to enrage them.

Oncidium orchids are pollinated by male *Centris* bees, which are extremely territorial and likely to respond to any kind of threat with hostility and aggression. By 'dancing' around in the breeze, *Oncidium* inflorescences (cluster of flowers) resemble a swarm of competitors. Eager to protect their territory, the bees attack the flowers, head first. On contact, the orchid's pollinium becomes attached to the bees' foreheads. The bees, upon spotting and charging at yet more 'rival swarms', transfer the pollinium from one *Oncidium* to the next, successfully pollinating the species and allowing for the continued survival of the very orchid that causes them so much anguish.

This style of pollination, although successful, is pretty unique among flowering plants and is one of our favourite examples of plant deception.

Angraecum and the Hawk Moth

Angraecum orchids are magnificent and rare. Their star-shaped white flowers look best in early evening when they light up and glow. They are sensitive orchids, which can make them tricky to grow indoors, but those who manage to find them extremely rewarding.

Angraecum sesquipedale is another of Darwin's favourites, so much so that it is commonly called 'Darwin's orchid'. Upon studying them, he surmised that the flowers must be pollinated by a moth with a long probiscis (tongue) due to the flowers' long nectar-bearing spurs, but such a moth was undiscovered in the natural world. As is often the way with Darwin's ahead-of-his-time theories, it was dismissed. Some 21 years after his death, however, he was proven right when they discovered *Xanthopan morganii praedicta*, mercifully nicknamed the 'hawk moth'. It has been suggested that the last name 'praedicta' was in honour of Darwin's prediction. The hawk moth is huge, with a 16-cm (6⅓-in) wingspan and a probiscis of at least 20 cm (8 in) which, when not in use, remains coiled up and tucked under its head.

The hawk moth is the perfect pollinator for the *A. sesquipedale* orchid, whose beautiful flowers contain a delicious reward. Similar to hummingbird-pollinated orchids, the flowers produce a long spur (reflected in the long probiscis of the hawk moth), which elongates back beyond the sex organs. Any insect or bird lucky enough to reach the back of the spur is rewarded with nectar.

The scent produced by *A. sesquipedale* attracts the hawk moth and lets it know the flower has nectar, and the hawk moth comes in close to the flower to make sure the scent belongs to the right species of orchid. Once sure of the species, the hawk moth backs up a foot or so before extending its long probiscis and flying forward to probe the flower. Once it's had its fill of nectar, the hawk moth lifts its head to remove the probiscis and, upon doing so, brushes against the plant's pollinium, which attaches to its head.

Once the hawk moth is finished, it flies away and repeats the process on another orchid, fertilising it in the process. Once pollinated, the orchid stops producing the scent, and the hawk moth knows it will not benefit from visiting the flower.

These species co-exist in perfect harmony, and it has been suggested they have evolved together. Some have theorised that the hawk moth has evolved to have the same length probiscis as the orchid's spur, so they don't have to fly too far from the flower when harvesting the nectar, reducing the risk of falling prey to tarantulas.

Darwin's prediction is a wonderful example of how an understanding of taxonomy and the physiology of plants – how they are pollinated and why they evolve to be the way they do – can lead to breakthroughs in science of the natural world. And although he was way ahead of his time, he instinctively knew. If he could see us today, he'd be saying a well-earned 'I told you so.'

DIVERSE AND DELIGHTFUL

Orchids are infamous and their value has unfortunately rocketed downwards. Many people no longer have the tolerance for them and associate them with the cellophane-wrapped orchids you find in a 2-for-1 deal at the supermarket. But in truth, they are so much more diverse and intelligent than we know. And their true beauty comes from their evolution and their history. We hope people can learn to appreciate this diverse family of plants as much as Darwin did and as much as they deserve.

Night Flowers

Native Locations
Mexico, The Amazon
Basin, Utah and
New Britain

"The moonflower is renowned as a treat for those who stroll through their gardens in the evening. Peeking open at night, almost as if they were seeking a rendezvous with the moon ..." —— Unknown

In the early evening, as the sun begins to set, many species of plant close their flowers, for fear of wasting energy while their pollinators are asleep. But it is at this time that a select few nocturnal angiosperms (flowering plants) create some of their most beautiful and sweet-smelling displays. Also known as 'moonflowers', night flowers are a relatively rare phenomenon, occurring in a small handful of angiosperms. Some night flowers appear for one night only before they fade and die, and some night flowers open and close continuously over a season until they are fertilised.

PLANTS THAT FLOWER AT NIGHT

This enchanting phenomenon occurs across a handful of plant species. The delicate flowers are a sight to behold, and it is not unknown for people to travel far to observe the occurrence in botanical gardens and horticultural displays, which will stay open late to mark the occasion. While many of the angiosperms who

practise night-flowering aren't commonly grown as houseplants, many can be grown either indoors or outdoors. There is one notable houseplant that does practise this incredible phenomenon: *Epiphyllum oxypetalum*, also known as a night-blooming cereus or 'queen of the night', is a houseplant related to *E. anguliger* or 'fishbone cactus'. *E. oxypetalum* is renowned for its beautiful night flowers, which, although rare, are a sure spectacle, and many houseplant cultivators purchase this species in the hopes of catching their beautiful, luminous night flowers (provided they can stay up late enough to observe them). As with many other species of night flower, the lone flower of *E. oxypetalum* lasts less than 12 hours, and so those who are lucky enough to spot a bud forming must be attentive and patient to witness the spectacle.

Strophocactus wittii is another plant which boasts night flowers, found growing epiphytically (on other plants or trees) in the flooded forest of the Amazon basin. This plant is perhaps the most common example of the phenomenon, so much so that it was adorned with the nickname 'Amazon moonflower'. The magical flowers bloom at sundown, producing a beautiful scent overnight, which turns rancid later on, and then they die once the light of the next day sets in. This species of night flower is commonly grown in botanical collections and gardens but is rarely grown as a houseplant due to its challenging growing requirements. In February 2021, the Cambridge University Botanic Garden saw the flowering of its own *Strophocactus wittii* and documented the incredible journey on its website. This gave botanists a chance to study the plant further and to witness the once-in-a-blue-moon occurrence.

Another species, which is rarely cultivated at home, but is often found in botanical collections, is *Datura innoxia*. This beautiful plant produces magnificent trumpet-shaped flowers in the early evening, which last throughout the night before closing back up mid-morning. These plants could be cultivated indoors, but they rarely are, because they are difficult to keep and are incredibly toxic. In many countries, the plant is banned due to its misuse and incidence of fatal poisonings. Of course, many houseplants we cultivate are toxic, but datura are infamous not only for their toxicity, but for their extremely hallucinogenic effects on humans. This is why many curious to try the effects fall victim to accidental overdose. A prime member of the deadly nightshade family, datura are nicknamed 'angel's trumpet' in reference to the perhaps enlightening, delirious side effects one might experience after consuming parts of their night flowers.

In 2011, botanists discovered a new species of orchid, *Bulbophyllum nocturnum*, so named because it is the first night-flowering orchid to have ever been discovered. The flowers of this orchid are small and pollinated by fungus gnats, which mistake the flowers for fungi. The botanists who discovered the orchid have speculated that it probably emits an odour, unnoticeable to humans, which smells like the fungus the gnats like to lay their eggs on. Why these orchids flower at night remains a mystery in the world of botany, but more and more studies of the plant are becoming available. Since this is a recent discovery, this orchid is not yet available on the plant market (and perhaps, due to its rarity in the wild, never will be), but it may be possible to find in botanic gardens in the coming years.

THE REASON BEHIND
THE PHENOMENON

While the idea of plants that bloom under the light of the moon is very romantic, these flowers, as all others do, serve a very real and practical purpose in the wild. Typically, flowers are pollinated by daytime pollinators, such as bees, flies, wasps and butterflies, which return to their nests in the early evening, and sleep, along with much of the rest of the world, during the night. Most plants use the pollinator-less night-time to close their flowers, saving themselves energy, conserving their scent and stopping their pollen from becoming wet in the morning dew. This closing of the flowers at night is known as nyctinasty.

If nyctinastic flowers close during the night-time due to a lack of pollinators, it stands to reason that night-flowering plants open up their flowers at twilight or in the early evening because this is when their pollinators are most active. In short: night flowers are pollinated by nocturnal pollinators. And while their pollinators are asleep during the day, the flowers have no reason to be open, so they close up.

So who pollinates the night flowers? It may come as a surprise to you to learn that bats are one of the most helpful pollinators during the night-time. Their ability to use echolocation, alongside their strong sense of smell, means that they find it relatively easy to locate night flowers, and they certainly enjoy the tasty nectar rewards for helping to complete the pollination cycle. Bats also help the plants further by feasting on predatory insects as a midnight snack. In fact, pregnant bats can fill themselves with up to 600 insects in a single night.

Another pollinator of the night flower is the hawkmoth. While the hawkmoth that visits the flowers of *Angraecum sesquipedale* (page 44) is not nocturnal, many species of hawkmoth are, and they are particularly attracted to large, fragrant white flowers. Hawkmoths have a long probiscis (tongue), which they unravel to dip into the nectar-filled tubes at the back of many species of night flowers. While they do so, they brush against the pollen. They then repeat the process with another night flower to complete the pollination cycle.

Sphynx moths are another well-documented pollinator of night flowers. These moths resemble hummingbirds, both in size and in their characteristic 'humming' sound. Sphynx moths tend to pollinate night-flowering plants in the Cactaceae (cactus) family, such as *S. wittii* and *E. oxypetalum*, whose long nectar tubes allow the sphynx moth to feed comfortably.

HELPING HAND TO POLLINATORS

At night-time or in the early evening, light levels are low and finding flowers to pollinate might prove difficult without a helping hand. And so plants that flower at night have developed a few flowery characteristics to help hawkmoths, the sphynx moth, bats and other night-time pollinators to locate flowers without too much difficulty. Firstly, the flowers these plants produce are usually big. The bigger the flower, the easier it is to locate during the evening hours. In some species, such as *E. oxypetalum*, the flowers can be as large as dinner plates, measuring around 15 cm (6 in) in diameter. Many species of night flowers are also very open, with petals stretching out from the edges of the flower, almost resembling an arrow pointing to the flower's centre. Most night-flowering plants also produce white or very pale flowers. Anyone who grows white flowers in the garden will know that they stick out like a sore thumb, especially at twilight. In the wild, the light from the moon will reflect off the white surface of the flower, creating a glowing beacon for pollinators that shouts, 'I'm here! Come and pollinate me!'

Since most nocturnal insects and mammals do not have keen eyesight, they may still struggle to locate the large, pale flowers, and so night-flowering plants have made things even easier for them. As many of us are aware, when one sense is dampened, the other senses are heightened – the same can be said for nocturnal animals. While they may struggle to see the flowers with such poor eyesight, they should be able to smell them. Plants that flower at night are usually extremely fragrant. Their sweet scent helps to guide pollinators in the right direction, while their large, shining flowers help the moth or bat zero in on their precise location. Perhaps the best example of powerful night-time fragrances can be observed in a jasmine plant. In the early evening, just as the sun is setting, jasmine emits a scent so powerful that even humans can smell it from afar, so imagine how potent and attractive it must be to a pollinator.

FINDING A MOONFLOWER

Most of us won't ever get to see night flowers in the wild, unless we go and seek them out for ourselves, but for those of us willing to spend a couple of pounds and wait, *E. oxypetalum* is a common houseplant that means we stand a small chance of enjoying this spectacle at home. We have never experienced the night flowers on this beautiful plant, but know a colleague who has. The photos were enough to send us reeling, and apparently the scent was divine.

CHAPTER 3

INSIDE PLANTS/ MEDICINAL

Euphorbia Sap

Native Locations
Southern Africa,
Madagascar, North
America, Turkey
and UK

"Many of these so-called bad plants ... contain incredible properties for healing or are necessary for some of the most magnificent wonders when combined with something else. Humans have a great capacity for declaring something good or evil, without truly knowing."

—— Wm. Paul Young, author

Euphorbiaceae is an enormous family of plants. It contains 300 genera and over 7,500 species, so covering it in its entirety would take years. In fact, it's the fifth largest family of flowering plants in the entire world, with species found almost everywhere across the globe and in an array of different forms (trees, shrubs, annuals, perennials, houseplants, weeds, etc.).

Some popular members of the Euphorbiaceae family include the infamous castor oil plant (*Ricinus communis*), made famous for producing the deadly compound ricin; the well-loved, colourful houseplant croton (*Codiaeum variegatum*); and the ever useful rubber tree (*Hevea brasiliensis*), the primary source of rubber throughout the world.

Although the plants included in this family are often collectively called 'euphorbia', this name actually only refers to one genus within this vast family. Known more commonly as 'spurge' or 'milkweed', *Euphorbia* is a massive genus of plants. It boasts more

than 2,000 different species, ranging from the desert-dwelling 'cacti' (page 56) bought from houseplant shops to ornamental garden plants and the rich red poinsettia gifted to loved ones during the holiday season. All those who've dipped their toes into the world of plants will have come across euphorbia at one time or another.

Being such a large genus of plants with so many species, there are certainly a vast array of topics deserving of coverage, but we're going to take a look at something we find fascinating: euphorbia sap. You may be wondering, is that it? But euphorbia sap is not just any old sap – it's infamous to those familiar with the plant and is invaluable to the survival of the genus.

The pointed truth

There are some discreet, but fundamental differences between a euphorbia 'cactus' and a true cactus. For example, the leaves of a true cactus have adapted over time to become pointed spines, both for water conservation and as protection from predators. Euphorbia 'cacti', on the other hand, produce true leaves, meaning their 'spines' are in fact thorns (like the thorns on a rosebush), serving no purpose other than protection. The second fundamental difference is … You guessed it, the sap. While both cacti and desert euphorbia store water for times of drought, true cacti do not produce sap, whereas euphorbia do.

Because both euphorbia 'cacti' and true cacti have evolved in the same environment, even though they might have grown up on entirely different continents; they have developed the same (or similar) adaptations in order to survive. This copycat behaviour is known as 'convergent evolution', and many species of plants around the world do the same thing (another good example of this is the production of caffeine in tea, coffee and cocoa plants).

TOXIC SAP

The first thing to touch on is the sap's toxicity. The sap can be found within all parts of a euphorbia plant. You can see it bleeding out as a milky-white latex when the plant is damaged, pruned, eaten or, in some delicate specimens, simply knocked.

People used to handling these plants are wary of the sap, and for very good reason: it contains a number of compounds and chemicals that work together to ward off predators – however, the toxic sap does not discriminate between predators and humans. If it comes into contact with your skin, it causes photosensitivity, meaning that skin becomes sensitive to sunlight and is easily burnt by UV rays, sometimes even to the extent of forming blisters. It also causes itching, irritation, redness and sometimes a burning sensation due to its caustic nature (Maddie can confirm these symptoms from her own gardening days, when she recklessly deadheaded a client's euphorbia).

Get it in your eyes and euphorbia sap can cause permanent blindness in the most extreme cases, and at the very least a bad bout of conjunctivitis. Luckily, most people recover within a few days with no long-term effects.

Ingestion of euphorbia sap, of course, is another matter entirely. We perish the thought anyone would try – although there are cases of mistaken identity where people have accidentally ingested the plant and, subsequently, the sap. There's a well-known legend passed around among horticulturalists and gardeners, whether or not it is true, it certainly serves as a warning.

The tale varies from person to person, but in essence it goes as follows: there was a man who ended up lost and stranded in the middle of a desert. With water supplies running low and dehydration inevitable, he decided to drink the water from a cactus. In a twist of unfortunate fate, the cactus he chose to drink from was not a cactus, but a euphorbia. The ingested sap formed ulcers and blisters inside his throat, and he died there and then, only to be discovered weeks later.

As with many urban legends, the origins of this story are uncertain, and we couldn't verify it. But it does highlight an important message: don't eat euphorbia.

This said, not all species within the euphorbia family are as toxic as one another. The sap in a *E. ingens* (the cowboy cactus many of us are familiar with at home), for example, is much more likely to cause severe reactions than the sap in a poinsettia.

Some studies of cattle that were unfortunate enough to graze on euphorbia found that poisoning differed massively depending on which species they grazed on. For example, cattle that grazed on poinsettia (*E. pulcherrima*) suffered only minor gastrointestinal upset (vomiting and diarrhoea), whereas cattle found grazing on the much more poisonous leafy spurge (*E. esula* – one of the most recognisable outdoor species) displayed symptoms such as irritation and blistering of the mouth and surrounding skin, salivation, bloody diarrhoea, vomiting and, in some cases, collapse and death.

Now, all of this might sound scary, and you may be wondering why humans bother to cultivate this plant at all, but one main purpose of the sap is to defend against predators, after all, so it has to be effective at doing its job. And for an immobile plant surrounded by potential predators and hungry herbivores, it does the trick fairly well.

SELF-HELP SEALANT

Aside from being a wonderful protection mechanism, the sap also works as an in-house doctor when defences fail. With a milky-white appearance and a watery texture (turning sticky on contact), the sap is best likened to the platelets in our blood when we get a cut: congealing, sealing and repairing as quickly as possible to avoid infection. The sap is held within the plant at high pressure, so when it does get damaged, the sap pours out, quickly flushing away any potential infectants before sealing the wound. The sap also contains antifungal and antibacterial properties, which further help to minimise the risk of disease after injury.

So for an *E. ingens*, for example, struggling to survive in an open, barren desert, its sap works as a lifeline. That's as long as it doesn't find itself being eaten by the aforementioned thirsty, lost man.

MEDICINAL MARVEL

Since the sap contains all of these defence mechanisms, it's unsurprising (as with many other toxic plants) that it's been used throughout medical history. A great deal of ancient remedies in Africa, India and China have used euphorbia sap in small doses to treat a number of different ailments. From wart removal to relief from sores and cracked heels, it contributed to many ancient remedies used in the treatment of skin diseases. *E. pugniformis*, which many (including Maddie) grow as an indoor succulent, has been used in India to treat indigestion, constipation, worms and other forms of gastric distress. *E. neriifolia*, occasionally called 'euphorbia of the ancients' (aptly named in accordance with its prehistoric look), is also commonly grown as an indoor succulent, and was used in ancient Indian medicine in the treatment of chest problems such as whooping cough and asthma.

Euphorbia are rarely used in Western medicine today. The adverse side effects, both from ingesting the plant and from direct skin contact, are difficult to regulate, and other medicines are readily available for the treatment of the conditions listed above. But in cultures where such Western medicine is less accessible or preferable, people have used euphorbia herbal remedies for thousands of years. They have had plenty of practise to perfect dosage and application, so the risk is low.

As houseplants, they vary in toxicity, and although it's best to keep any euphorbia plants away from young children and pets, some are undeniably safer than others. Poinsettia (*E. pulcherrima*), for example, is probably the least toxic of all the species, only producing mild symptoms on contact – while the pencil cactus (*E. tirucalli*) is one of the most (if not the most) toxic species within the genus and can cause severe symptoms. Other species we cultivate indoors include *E. ingens*, *E. trigona*, *E. tetra* and *E. triangularis*. These are the species we often falsely label as cacti.

Wherever – and in whatever circumstances – a euphorbia crosses your path, we hope you'll have a new-found respect for this immensely fascinating plant – and might even consider growing one for yourself (just remember not to eat it).

Aloe Vera

Native Locations
Sudan and the
Arabian Peninsula

Aloe vera is certainly the standout species of its genus. Its name as familiar to many of us as a rose is in the cut flower world. Across the globe, it's adored for its minimal care needs, architectural beauty and, the reason we're here today, its many health and healing benefits.

At the moment, you're more likely to find *Aloe vera* on the market (outside of the plant industry) in the form of popular soft drinks, where the fleshy gel has been mixed with water and flavoured, or as an ultra-healthy aloe shot to aid digestion. But if you dig a little deeper, you should be able to find single leaves sold on market stands and in certain supermarkets. And what's the bonus of having the raw stem? Well, you can use it for any one of its healing properties. You can, of course, grow *Aloe vera* at home in a sunny and dry enough spot. But if you're planning on harvesting the leaves, you might want to have a few plants on the go to ensure you have a regular supply and give the plants time to produce new growth.

HEALING AROUND THE WORLD

While the exact origin of *Aloe vera* is the source of much debate, especially since it's now been so widely transplanted across the globe, research has suggested that Sudan and the Arabian Peninsula are

a likely bet. You'll now find them growing pretty much anywhere there is some sunshine and even the smallest amount of soil beneath an undesirable surface: the deserts of South America, tropical and southern Africa, arid areas of the Mediterranean, and islands across the Indian Ocean, just for starters! Perhaps it has travelled so far afield because of its almost-magical healing properties. Even those living thousands of years ago cherished the benefits this plant provides. And luckily, even with the wonders of modern medicine, we haven't forgotten how amazing it truly is.

FOR THE SKIN

Chances are you've come across a moisturiser or skin treatment containing aloe, and for good reason! There are so many benefits to using it on our skin that it's a wonder we aren't all growing *Aloe vera* in abundance to smother ourselves in their all-healing gel.

Aloe vera is packed full of vitamins, enzymes, amino acids and many other compounds that are effective in healing cuts, grazes and minor burns. Its molecular structure helps to heal wounds quickly while minimising scarring. It does this by boosting collagen levels and fighting bacteria. The cooling and moisturising nature of the gel works wonders as an aftersun treatment as well as a salve on minor burns. In fact, early studies have shown that it is a more effective sun treatment than some mainstream burn creams on the market and will provide faster pain relief and allow the burns to heal more quickly. It also contains a wealth of anti-inflammatory properties helpful for soothing insect bites, stings and rashes.

Moving over to the beauty industry, the use of *Aloe vera* in skincare products has become ever more abundant. Many of the properties used in wound ailment are also what make it a popular choice here. While its presence in skincare is no new phenomenon, it is only recently that it seems to have appeared at the forefront of marketing campaigns and become a major selling point for the brands using it. Natural skincare is something that many of us are starting to prioritise, and this wonder ingredient is an all-rounder for treating a whole host of concerns, so it's no suprise that it's the go-to plant.

Aloe vera gel absorbs very easily, so is great for those of us with oily skin. However, it is also deeply moisturising and nourishing and can be used on both dry and sensitive skin types. As we've mentioned previously, it's full of anti-inflammatory compounds. This makes it ideal to help treat inflammatory forms of acne, such as pustules and nodules. Components in the gel called polysaccharides and gibberellins help to stimulate the generation of new cells while reducing redness and swelling. It also has astringent properties (those that cause contraction of skin cells), which will reduce the size of pores and the excess production of sebum, preventing future outbreaks. Finally, although it's not widely acknowledged as an anti-ageing ingredient, the fact that it's known to boost collagen levels surely makes it a strong contender in the arena, but we will let you come to your own conclusions on that one.

INTERNAL AIDS

Next up are the plant's all-important but unseen internal healing properties. The benefits of drinking *Aloe vera* are as broad and exciting as the impact it can have on our skin and face. The amino acids, vitamins and minerals that help us with external healing do just as much good to our internal organs – and have been known to soothe or even cure some symptoms of chronic conditions such as IBS if taken regularly.

Even if you don't suffer from a stomach ailment, it's well worth taking shots of aloe vera gel to help strengthen and detoxify your body from the inside. The anti-inflammatory and antibacterial properties are a great digestion aid and are fantastic for keeping up the health of your gut. *Aloe vera* may even help inhibit the growth of *H. pylori* bacteria, which is found in your digestive tract and can lead to ulcers. It helps along the growth of good bacteria in the gut, in turn keeping digestive disorders at bay.

Having taken aloe shots regularly, we can safely say it isn't the tastiest of health shots you'll find, but slip one into a fresh juice or smoothie in the morning and you won't even know you've had it. Having said that, it's probably worth noting that *Aloe vera* can have a laxative effect, especially if taken in large quantities, so make sure to have no more than a small shot daily.

It is also helpful at keeping your oral health and hygiene in check. The same properties that aid in gut health are also extremely good at fighting the build-up of plaque and general debris in the mouth. *Aloe vera* is proven to have as much, if not more, effect on plaque levels as mainstream brands, and therefore lowers the chances of resulting problems, such as gum disease and tooth rot. Who would have thought it? Although the taste of *Aloe vera* isn't particularly appealing, you'll find more aloe mouthwash brands emerging with flavours that will leave you minty fresh.

A DROP IN THE OCEAN

We've mentioned plenty of the health and beauty benefits of *Aloe vera*, but we probably haven't even touched the surface. People across the globe have different ways of using the plant to treat ailments of all levels of severity; some are medically proven and some are traditions proven by the test of time. Either way, we are sure you can agree that this really is a wonder plant that, although common, should certainly not be overlooked. Sometimes our familiarity with something can make us dismissive of it, but hopefully we've given you plenty of reasons to think a little more about how extraordinary this commonplace beauty really is.

"I believe the 21st century will confirm Aloe vera to be the greatest medicine mankind has ever known."

—

Lee Ritter, N.D.,
Doctor of Naturopathy

Kalanchoe

Native Location
Tropical Africa

Kalanchoe is a genus of succulent plants native to tropical Africa (namely Madagascar), but they have become widely cultivated and therefore naturalised in many tropical and subtropical regions across the globe, including Central and South America, Hawaii and Australia, to name a few. Although they can be found worldwide, it's in the Caribbean and West Indies that their use in medicinal culture is the most prominent.

Many species can be used medicinally, but *K. pinnata*, *K. daigremontiana* and *K. integra* are most commonly grown for this purpose. There are a vast number of ways they can be prepared to treat a long list of ailments, making them a staple plant in Caribbean households. Luckily, these species are not only easy to grow because of their drought-tolerant and forgiving nature but also extremely easily propagated, so expanding your collection can be done without too much thought.

PROPAGATION SPREADS THE BENEFITS

While you can force propagation easily, most kalanchoe plants self-propagate so frequently and readily that you most likely won't need to start the process yourself. When the original plant is placed

directly onto soil, plantlets start to form along the serrated edge of certain kalanchoe leaves. Once these plantlets are well established (you should be able to tell if roots have formed by giving them a gentle tug, looking for some light resistance), you can plant each one into its own pot, ready to grow into an established plant full of medicinal wonders! Other varieties, such as 'mother of thousands' (*K. daigremontiana*), will start growing plantlets on the edges of their leaves before they've even fallen, meaning that when the plantlets drop, they're already partially formed and simply need to root themselves into the soil.

Leaves on certain species of kalanchoe will often grow quite large and become too heavy for their thin stem to hold, particularly because of the foliage's dense, succulent make-up. Kalanchoe are also brittle, so the leaves will fall easily when knocked or brushed past. In the wild, although the main purpose of the waxy foliage is to store and retain water in preparation for times of drought, dropping the leaves (which often results in self-propagation) is how the species ensures its survival.

In the home, it is usually more effective to propagate kalanchoe by stem-cutting rather than using the leaves, as the former method tends to produce stronger plants and the cuttings will root faster. This method of propagation is done by cutting off a stem or branch (one without a flower) that's at least 5–8 cm (2–3 in) in length and removing its lower leaves, making sure to leave at least one pair of leaves at the top of the stem. Put the cutting aside for a few days to allow it to callous (dry out at the cut end). Once calloused, simply stick the end an inch or so into a pot filled with free-draining compost that has been lightly dampened and place the pot into a spot with bright but indirect light. Once the cutting has rooted, you should start to see new leaves forming, but if you're unsure, a light tug on the stem should be met with a little resistance once roots are formed.

If you want to propagate your kalanchoe in water (this will allow roots to form *before* being potted into soil), you take the same cutting but instead of leaving it to callous, stick it straight into a jar filled with water and wait for roots to grow to around twice the length of the bare stem.

Although it might seem inefficient to use the leaves of a single plant grown in the home for its medicinal values, the ease of propagation means that you'll likely have replacement plants already growing before you've had a chance to devour the parent. They are also a mostly pest- and disease-free plant, especially when grown indoors, so make very easy-going house guests.

HEALING PROPERTIES:
BURNS, BOILS AND BITES

There are many components that contribute to the healing benefits of kalanchoe, each of which can be brought out by different methods of preparation, including its antihistamine and anti-inflammatory properties. These components include tannins (commonly used to treat skin disorders), flavonoids (which help your body function more efficiently while protecting it against everyday toxins and stressors), and a multitude of vitamins, which we won't bore you with the details of here. Instead, we will talk a little about the most common methods of preparation and how those familiar with the plant use it to treat common ailments.

Kalanchoe plants can be used medicinally in two ways – they can be either ingested or applied to the skin, depending on what they're being used to treat. It is typically the main body of the plant that's used (the leaves and stems) rather than the roots and flowers. The most common way to ingest a kalanchoe is by boiling the leaves and drinking the residual water as a tea (this can be done with dried leaves as well as fresh). The newly softened leaves can then be kept to use directly on the skin (page 70). You can also cook the stems and leaves to eat in soups. Eating or drinking kalanchoe is used as a natural treatment for many internal ailments and illnesses, including (but not limited to): internal inflammation and infections, diarrhoea, diabetes, kidney stones, arthritis, menstrual disorders, epilepsy, asthma, bronchitis, cholera, urinary problems, cancer, IBS, intestinal problems, stomach bugs, allergies, colds and flus. Quite the list!

Alternatively, the leaves and stems can be crushed and applied to the skin directly to treat external ailments. Used in this way, kalanchoe can treat ailments such as wounds to the surface layers of skin, ulcers, abscesses, burns, inflammation, swelling, boils, insect bites and rashes. As mentioned above, the leaves which have been boiled to make tea can be saved for use on the skin, although this is better for treating milder ailments, such as insect bites, because it will be slightly diluted, so the effects are weakened.

THE MIRACLE LEAF

With such an extensive list of healing properties, combined with their simple and minimal care needs and easy propagation methods, this plant's popularity is certainly not without merit. In the UK, there are certain varieties that are frequently overlooked because of their association with the 1970s (hello, grandparents' plant collection!) or because they can be found in most garden centres, DIY stores and even supermarkets around the country. But now you know all the benefits of owning a kalanchoe, you might look at them a little differently and perhaps even consider getting one for yourself. We are huge fans of the almost alien appearance *K. daigremontiana* adds to a plant collection, so be sure to keep your eyes peeled for it and more unusual varieties!

"Nature itself is the best physician."

—

Hippocrates II,
physician

Can you eat
your houseplants?

Well, the honest answer here is no. We really don't advise it. And we certainly wouldn't want to induce any accidental poisonings. But that doesn't mean that they aren't used for food and medicines elsewhere. With the right knowledge and understanding of growing and preparing them to be used for consumption, many of the plants we have at home can, in fact, be eaten!

Most of the houseplants we buy are grown for ornamental use, meaning they're often sprayed with pesticides and chemicals to keep them in optimal condition. But in parts of the world where our houseplants are naturally found growing, they will have been used for centuries as consumables and are therefore grown and farmed on the basis they will be used for that purpose, as well as for their ornamental value. Many of the plants we talk about in this section have only been cultivated on the European market very recently, but in their native habitats they're as commonplace and normal to use for food as something like a blackberry bush might be in the UK.

MEDICINAL USE

As well as being eaten, many plants are used for their medicinal properties. Some houseplants, such as the *Aloe vera* (page 60), are well known for their health benefits and healing properties, and they are often bought on the European market because of these. But there are many more common household medicines we use that derive from plants we don't keep indoors.

Aspirin is something many of us have at home, and is widely used for both its pain-relieving and blood-thinning properties. Aspirin derives from the willow, a type of tree or shrub that grows across most of the globe. Its bark has been used for thousands of

years to treat headaches and back pain. The bark contains an active ingredient called salicin, which is an important component in the make-up of aspirin, but is still used today, unprocessed, as a natural alternative for pain relief.

Another plant-derived medicine many of us know (although probably don't keep at home) is morphine, an opiate derived from the opium poppy (*Papaver somniferum*). Opium poppies, although not kept as houseplants, are often bought as cut flowers and can be found growing in gardens across the globe. Poppy seeds are also commonly used in baked goods, such as bread and sweet treats like cakes. Although your poppy-seed bagel won't induce an opiate high, if the seeds are consumed in large enough quantities, they can be known to give a false positive in drug tests.

OPUNTIA

Although we keep many varieties of *Opuntia* as houseplants, *O. ficus-indica* is the one typically used for eating. It is generally thought that *O. ficus-indica* is native to the rocky and arid regions of Mexico, but it can now be found growing anywhere in the world that will provide the right conditions, including the Mediterranean, the Middle East, North Africa and Australia, where it is often considered an invasive weed.

This tasty desert-dweller, which you might know by its more common name, prickly pear, has been cultivated for food production for thousands of years, with some archaeological evidence proving links back to ancient civilisations, particularly the Aztecs. It has also long been used as cattle fodder, providing not only a tasty meal for the cattle but also acting as an escape-deterring spiked fence. Every part of the *O. ficus-indica* is edible, and the fruit and other parts of the plant (used as vegetables) are now cultivated and consumed in many other countries where the climate suits. It can be found in food shops worldwide (although you might have to do a little searching). The fruit, which usually follows after a glorious and long-lasting flower, remains on the plant until removed by humans, birds or animals. The animals that eat it excrete the seeds, which is how *O. ficus-indica* spreads in the wild. The fruit, often likened in taste to a watermelon, is actually a berry with a high sugar content and low acidity levels, and contains high amounts of vitamin E, carotenoids, dietary fibre, amino acids and antioxidants. The nutritional value (and extreme tastiness) of these berries goes a long way to explaining their popularity through the ages. It's definitely one to try if you find it in a shop near you.

COLOCASIA ESCULENTA (TARO)

Colocasia esculenta is a tropical plant that is most often referred to as taro, which is also what it's known as in its edible form. It is of the same family (Araceae) as monstera and alocasia, the latter of which many liken it to (particularly the *Alocasia amazonica* variety) because of the two plants' extremely similar appearance. Although colocasia are not often kept as houseplants, many people grow them in their gardens, even in cooler and less humid climates under glass or in pots on a sheltered patio.

Taro is one of the most ancient cultivated crops and although the conclusion has been made that it likely originated in southern India or South East Asia, it remains unclear. Regardless, it has now been naturalised across the globe and its corm (a bulbous sort of modified root) is as widely consumed as other root vegetables with a similar diversity, such as the potato or yam.

Taro root is a staple crop in West Africa, with Nigeria becoming the biggest producers of taro (known there as 'cocoyam' or 'arrowroot') in the world. The sweet and nutty root can be baked or roasted, but it's often boiled and the water kept as tea.

Although the root is the most commonly eaten part of the plant, young taro leaves can be eaten too. They are boiled twice to improve flavour and texture, and are full of protein and both vitamins A and C.

While you aren't likely to get hold of the leaves as easily in the West, you should be able to find taro at your local greengrocer's.

Why not give it a go in place of potatoes next time? Then perhaps you'll feel encouraged to grow them at home, too.

OXALIS

Oxalis is a genus with many species, cultivars and varieties, most of which are not commonly kept as house or garden plants. Instead, they're often regarded as a common weed due to their invasive, spreading nature. However, there are a few ornamental species, such as the *O. triangularis*, which are favourites among many and can be kept both indoors and out.

Oxalis can be found growing in most places around the world, but the species diversity is prolific in Brazil, Mexico and South Africa. While we can't be sure that this is how their edible properties were discovered, perhaps the best way to get rid of any invasive weed is to eat it.

Both the leaves and tubers of oxalis are edible, although in extremely large quantities they can be toxic. Despite the fact the risk of poisoning is highly unlikely and extremely rare, eating oxalis should still be avoided if you're pregnant or suffering from kidney problems. They're widely used across the globe and have been for centuries, both for medicinal purposes and as a food source. Native Americans used to chew the leaves on long trips to quench their thirst, while Native Canadians considered oxalis an aphrodisiac. In New Zealand, they continue to cultivate and sell the roots as 'New Zealand yam'. Historically, these plants were used to treat many ailments, including scurvy, fevers and sore throats. Although we have (thankfully) moved on in modern medicine, they are still used today as a natural alternative to cold and fever treatments.

One of the most common ways oxalis is used now is in food, where the colourful leaves and flowers (particularly those of the *O. triangularis* species) are often eaten raw in salads or as garnish for meat and fish. Both the flowers and the leaves are likened in taste to lemon because of their sour taste, which comes from oxalic acid, a compound named after the plant. This acid is the reason some medical professionals might advise against eating oxalis in large quantities, but the amount is only the same as you would find in spinach or rhubarb, which we eat in abundance.

YUCCA

Yucca is a large genus native to the arid regions of Central America, South America and the Caribbean where they stand sturdy in the harshest of desert conditions, experiencing dry heat, prolonged periods of drought and intense sunlight. In such difficult conditions, it is always helpful when an ornamental beauty like this doubles up as a food source.

A yucca's fruits, flowers and seeds are edible and can be eaten raw as a component in salads, or used as garnish in drinks or on cakes. The flowers can also be boiled and the water used as a tea, but they must be picked at just the right time to ensure optimal flavour. In their prime, the flowers taste a bit like asparagus or artichoke, which is not so surprising when you realise they come from the Asparagaceae family.

The fruit, although commonly eaten when available, is rare to come across. It is usually roasted or baked and is similar in taste to a fig, hence its use in salads and sweets.

The yucca's trunk and roots aren't edible, but they're extremely fibrous in nature and often used as a craft material for making paper and weaving baskets, adding to the overall usefulness for those living in the plant's natural habitats. The yucca is not to be confused with the similarly named yuca (also known as cassava), the roots of which are used widely in cooking. There is a high presence of a toxic compound called saponin in yucca roots, which is antibacterial and antifungal, and creates a lather. It's commonly used as soap but is an irritant if ingested.

FOOD FOR THOUGHT

Although 'Can I eat this?' is not something we're asked often about houseplants, it's a question we felt we wanted to answer, *just* in case anyone was wondering ... There are, of course, many more 'houseplants' that are, or have historically been, consumed across the globe (page 8 to find out about the delicious *Monstera deliciosa* fruit, and page 60 to read more on the healing properties of *Aloe vera*), but hopefully we have spiked your curiosity enough for you to go forth and discover more.

Although this still doesn't mean you can eat the plants in your house (for the prior reasons stated) unless you've *really* done your research and are confident you know what you're doing, we would certainly encourage trying them out if you come across them on the menu in areas of the world where they are endemic. If they are prepared by someone who knows best, you're bound to experience them in their full glory and get a tasty reminder of your experience whenever you see them at home.

"A person who is growing a garden, if he is growing it organically, is improving a piece of the world. He is producing something to eat, which makes him somewhat independent of the grocery business, but he is also enlarging, for himself, the meaning of food and the pleasure of eating."

—

Wendell Berry,
writer, farmer and environmental activist

CHAPTER 4

IN CULTURE

Bromeliads

Native Locations
Tropical Americas,
American sub-tropics
(e.g. Florida) and
Tropical West Africa

"We are all richer for biodiversity." —— **Stephen Fry**, actor

Bromeliads (plants within the Bromeliaceae family) are often overlooked by houseplant lovers – perhaps because we've become so accustomed to them; but, from tank bromeliads in the rainforest to sheep-eating bromeliads in Peru, it's safe to say Bromeliaceae is a hugely diverse family of plants. And with their evolutionary splendour, it would be almost offensive to ignore them in this book.

Nowadays, bromeliads are so readily available that their life in the natural world is hard to imagine. Although made popular as a basic, easy-care houseplant, the true nature of a bromeliad and their symbiosis with the wildlife in their natural habitat is seldom acknowledged; unfortunately, this lack of understanding has helped to lessen their value over time.

With over 3,500 individual species, bromeliads are one of the largest families in South America, so it's unsurprising it has found its way into our lives. While air plants and Spanish moss are surprising members of this broad family of plants, perhaps the most unexpected member is the pineapple. For those more familiar with bromeliads, the texture, colour and shape of the leaves which sprout from the top of the fruit is, for many, a recognisable characteristic (bar the flowering bracts) of the diverse family.

BROMELIADS: A BRIEF HISTORY

Long before bromeliads were introduced to Europe for cultivation, they played an integral part of daily life for the Mayans, the Incas and the Aztecs of South America. They used them as a source of food and medicine (both for themselves and cattle), and weaved hammocks and nets and made string and yarn for clothing from their fibres.

In the 1500s, Spanish conquistadors introduced the pineapple (*Ananas comosus*) to Europe. Having rarely been exposed to such exotic luxuries, many horticulturalists coveted the pineapple. From pineapple embellishments in masonry and appearances in artwork and sculptures to the rise in popularity of 'pineapple houses' (specifically designed for use in tropical plant cultivation in cold climates) on rural estates in the 1700s, the exotic fruit quickly became symbolic of wealth and status. Many stone walls within old stately homes in Europe are still embellished with pineapples today.

In 1776, *Guzmania lingulata* (perhaps the most recognisable bromeliad besides the pineapple) was introduced to Europe, causing a sensation among gardeners and exotic plant cultivators. With a beautiful, exotic reddish-orange set of bracts crowning it, and hidden flowers within, the plant mesmerised people.

It wasn't until the mid-Victorian era, around 50 years later, that the craze for bromeliads gained a new lease of life. In 1828, another (now remarkably common) bromeliad captivated the world of European exotic plant growers: *Aechmea fasciata*. Nothing of the like had been seen before, with large, enveloping silvery leaves, a spiky soft-pink bract and royal-purple gem-like flower buds peppering the gaps in the bracts. Perhaps this image no longer has the capacity to excite the modern houseplant grower, but to the average European in the 1800s, *Aechmea fasciata* was an alien plant with unknown properties and striking features. The silvery shimmer cast by the leaves made this bromeliad even more popular than the (dull by comparison) *Guzmania sp.*

Around 20 years later, *Vriesea splendens* (another popular species grown today) was introduced to Europe and, once again, caused a sensation. This time, it was due to the natural variegation on the leaves, which had deep green and purple zebra-like stripes, and a tall, rounded red bract.

In the late 19th century, breeders in Belgium, the Netherlands and France began hybridising bromeliads for wholesale, and suddenly a whole new market of cultivars became available for amateurs and experts alike. Despite the popularity of new varieties and hybrids, which nobody had ever seen before, *Guzmania linguilata*, *Aechmea fasciata* and *Vriesea splendens* are still among the most popular bromeliads sold today.

WHERE BROMELIADS GROW

Bromeliads come in a variety of different shapes and sizes, and grow in a number of different places across the globe. Around half of the 3,500 known species of bromeliads are epiphytic, which means they grow on other plants and trees (in a non-parasitic fashion). Most epiphytic bromeliads can be found growing naturally and in abundance in the tropics and subtropics of the Americas; places like Brazil, Jamaica, Costa Rica and Ecuador are host to many of these species.

Several terrestrial bromeliads (those growing in the ground) can be found in arid and semi-arid climates within the Americas, such as Peru, Bolivia and other countries that border the Andes. Some genera of bromeliad, such as *Tillandsia* sp. (which includes Spanish moss and other air plants) contain such a broad range of species that they can be found growing naturally from North Carolina, USA, all the way down to Mexico, and further south.

Generally speaking, bromeliads grow wherever they can, and are usually un-fussy about their living quarters. This is because they derive most of their nutrients from the water and rotting organic matter (from their surrounding habitat) that collects within their leaves. Bromeliads can also be lithophytic (growing on rocks and stones). The bromeliads we cultivate for indoor use tend to be either epiphytic or lithophytic.

Epiphytic bromeliads are often found in the wild residing high up in the biggest trees, clinging onto the tallest branches in the canopy layer of the rainforest; this gives them access to bright light and plenty of water, as well as an abundance of falling leaf litter and other organic matter, which they use as a source of nutrients. In less densely packed ecosystems, bromeliads can be found collecting en masse in the brightest parts of large trees, where they are able to harvest the most sunlight. Bromeliads are also more commonly found growing on older trees, as there tend to be more supporting nooks and crannies to grow in.

Lithophytic bromeliads can be found growing in any rocky terrain. Some can be found high up in windy, dry, mountainous habitats, growing through cracks or attaching themselves to rocks, which they use as a source of minerals.

Interestingly, it is thought that terrestrial (earth-dwelling) bromeliads were around long before their epiphytic or lithophytic counterparts. The roots of any terrestrial plant serve a multitude of functions, but two of the most important are the harvesting of water and nutrients from the soil. However, over time, the densely packed leaves of terrestrial bromeliads became much more adequate at holding and harvesting water and nutrients than the roots, rendering the roots near-obsolete. Since the bromeliads were so successful at finding water and nutrient sources outside of the soil, future seeds were able to settle on structures such as trees and boulders, using their roots for stability only.

LIFE ALONGSIDE ANIMALS
AND WILDLIFE

Bromeliads, while beautiful, are also extremely functional plants, and with a history dating back more than 60 million years, they've had a lot of time to perfect their physiology. Now they have an essential synergy with, and significant impact on, surrounding wildlife in their natural habitats. Epiphytic bromeliads cover more than half of all plants within the Bromeliaceae family and are often found in trees, safely nestled on the highest branches in the canopy layer of rainforests in tropical climates.

Physiologically, perhaps the best asset to any bromeliad is its leaves. Tightly packed together at the base of the plant, they create a water-tight vessel which serves as a phytotelma (a naturally occurring pool of freshwater that collects in or on plants). Some species of bromeliad are aptly nicknamed 'tank bromeliads' because they can hold as much as 20 litres (5 gallons) of water within their leaves.

The pools that collect in the leaves act as a wildlife haven for a number of different species that live alongside the bromeliads in the canopy. Amphibians, such as frogs, and insects, like damselfly and mosquitos, lay their eggs within the water; although doing so in such an open nursery can come at a price. Some species of crustacean, such as the bromeliad crab, do away with any competition to ensure the survival of their own protégé. They kill off the damselfly larvae and lay their own eggs in their place. Insect larvae also often fall victim to the tadpoles of poison dart frogs. The frogs lay their eggs among other leaves, then, when their eggs hatch into tadpoles, the mother frog transports them on her back to bromeliad pools where there is an abundance of food in the form of insect eggs or algae.

FOOD, DRINK AND A PLACE TO HIDE

An array of other animals also rely on the bromeliad pools as sources of food and water. Mammals such as shrews, lemurs and small monkeys can be found drinking from the leaves, while some species of salamander, scorpion, snake and lizard visit the pools, using them as a vending machine to snack on some eggs or have a drink of water.

Dried-out leaves make a nice hiding spot for spider species, from jumping spiders to tarantulas. They use the leaves to conceal themselves before pouncing on an unsuspecting victim. And with all the other animals and insects that visit the pools, there is a lot of prey around.

For all the larger living organisms that benefit from the pools of vitality, there are a great number of tiny, even microscopic, species who also get a lot from the bromeliads. Many species of algae, protozoa, and even miniature carnivorous plants called bladderworts live within the pools, feeding off bacteria and other microscopic plants and insects.

Unfortunately, the pools sometimes attract insects that are harmful to humans. In Brazil, they are host to anopheles. These mosquitos are infamous and responsible for a great number of malaria cases in humans. Since many species within the *Anopheles* genus rely on the phytotelma of bromeliads to complete their lifecycle, in 1942 local programmes of bromeliad eradication were implemented in regions where malaria was prevalent to try and eliminate the disease. These bromeliad pools are essential to the life of a great many animals and insects living in the rainforest biomes – without them, the balance would be quickly disrupted. One study, in the Ecuadorian lowlands, found over 11,200 organisms, representing more than 300 distinct species, living within the phytotelmas created by only 209 bromeliads. Some of these species lived exclusively within the natural pools, surely a testament to the necessity of these tiny ecosystems.

CARNIVOROUS BROMELIADS?

One species of bromeliad (*Puya chilensis*) has been accused of ensnaring sheep and self-fertilising with the remains, in a kind of protocarnivorous act. The carnivorous Venus flytrap, when its trap is activated, snaps shut and hermetically seals all escape routes before producing a soup of digestive secretions within its leaves, allowing the plant to digest its prey and reabsorb the nutrient-rich fluid. Since Venus flytraps grow in nutrient-poor soil, this process is essential in keeping them well fed, making sure they are able to grow and reproduce. Protocarnivorous plants, on the other hand, may be able to trap insects and animals, but don't have the physiological means of directly absorbing nutrients from their carcasses. They do benefit from their decomposition, and the nutritional value they provide to the plant, but it isn't essential to the continued survival of their species.

Puya chilensis are among the largest species of bromeliad in the world. With long, strap-like barbed leaves and flowers often reaching over 6 metres (20 feet) in height, these terrestrial bromeliads can be found growing in large clusters on the dry hillsides of Chile, where a number of animals graze on the surrounding grass. In such a dry and unforgiving climate, being a large plant comes with a great number of disadvantages; the bigger the plant, the more nutrients necessary to keep it alive and thriving. And in these circumstances, the potential for protocarnivory could be extremely useful.

Using the only tools they have – their barbed leaves and large size – *Puya chilensis*, growing side by side and en masse, ensnare the peacefully grazing sheep (among other unfortunate animals). The sheep's wool gets caught in the barbed leaves and, as they fight to escape, they tangle themselves into an increasingly worse position until they become well and truly stuck. Utterly unable to free themselves, they slowly suffer from dehydration or malnutrition, and eventually die. The resulting decomposition of the sheep provides the soil surrounding the bromeliads with a rich fertiliser, which they absorb through their far-reaching roots.

The ensnarement of the sheep is massively beneficial and perhaps even crucial to the life of these bromeliads. *Puya chilensis* could be the perfect example of protocarnivory, provided it can be proven that the plant traps the sheep on purpose.

Whether this was a conscious evolutionary adaptation is up for debate, however, and scientists aren't wholly in agreement. Some who have studied the plant and its unusual relationship with Chilean sheep, don't count this as protocarnivorous behaviour, while others say it is a prime example. To us, whether or not the plants do it on purpose, the concept is exciting, and we like to think of it as an enthusiastic lust for survival in a less than sympathetic habitat.

Ficus Elastica

Native Locations
Indonesia, Malaysia,
India, China and Nepal

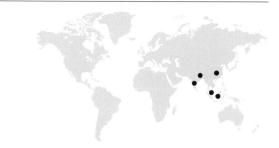

Ficus elastica, known by most as a rubber plant, rubber fig or an Indian rubber tree, is perhaps one of the most cultivated houseplants, and in warm climates it is often grown outdoors as an ornamental tree. The plant is native to many countries across Asia, including Indonesia, Malaysia, India, China and Nepal – but has been naturalised in most tropical and subtropical countries across the globe. The plants have long been popular in houseplant cultivation since they are easy to grow and propagate, and they fill a dull room with ease. The plants are also extremely durable.

As a houseplant, *Ficus elastica* is relatively unremarkable, bearing woody stems and oval green leaves – although there are many cultivars on the market which make this plant a bit more interesting, including 'Tineke', a pink and pale green blotchy cultivar (which looks a bit like pink camouflage print), and 'Abidjan', a dark purple cultivar with pink undersides and a bright red midrib (central vein). Since the plants rarely grow to be bigger than our homes allow in cultivation, it can be hard to imagine them growing in the wild – where their tremendous size and impressively sculptural growth habit can be truly appreciated. In the wild, *Ficus elastica* are almost unrecognisable; they can grow to be 100 metres (328 feet) tall, with incredible dangling roots, which can grow to form perfectly straight, strong pillars, and twisting, sculptural trunks.

ROOTED ABOVE GROUND

Aerial roots, in their simplest form, are roots which grow above ground. These can grow from branches or across stems and there is an array of different types, including the clinging roots of an epiphytic bromeliad (page 82) and the adventitious roots of a monstera (page 8) or of a ficus. These adventitious roots (meaning those that are produced in an unusual part of a plant) grow once the ficus has reached full maturity and serve the purpose of supporting the plant and keeping it stable as its canopy grows ever bigger. These types of adventitious roots are known as 'prop roots', since they 'prop' the plant up as it grows. The same prop roots can be observed (on a much smaller scale) on *Zea mays*, or sweetcorn plants.

As the rubber plant reaches maturity in the wild, it begins to produce an army of thin and flimsy aerial roots from its branches, which race down from the tree, acting as a stabiliser once they reach the soil. Upon contact with the soil, the roots quickly thicken and solidify, becoming almost trunk-like in thickness and appearance. Over time, it becomes difficult to discern between the tree's aerial roots and the tree itself. As the roots fall, they often become entwined, giving the appearance of multiple trees growing around one another. This leaves the singular tree with a mystical forest vibe. It is through the formation of these aerial roots that the following phenomenon occurs.

LIVING BRIDGES

For people living in the climates and countries where rubber plants grow naturally, the roots can be extremely useful to everyday life, especially since they grow so quickly. The state of Meghalaya in India has the highest level of rainfall in the country (it is thought that some areas see the highest levels of rain on earth). As such, the hills and mountains are covered in dense, subtropical rainforest. Endless streams of running water filter through the forest, creating deep ravines, crevices and gorges until the water spills from the hills in heaving waterfalls. The plant life surrounding these pools of vitality is thick and abundant, and the state boasts a significant number of native plants, birds and other animals. The rare pitcher plants *Nepenthes khasiana* (page 148) are endemic to this region, and the hills are home to more than 350 species of orchid. The area is also replete with minerals and geological formations.

Within the hills, among the animals and rich plant life, there are a collection of isolated villages and towns, where the tribal Khasi, Garo and Jaintia people (often referred to collectively as the Khasi people) have made their home. Together, these towns and villages are known as the Garo-Khasi-Jaintia range but are often simply referred to as the Khasi Hills. Some areas within the Meghalaya rainforest are kept protected as 'sacred groves', due to the matrilineal tribes' religious and cultural beliefs. This conservation is what has fuelled the infrastructural wonder of the 'living bridges of Meghalaya'. The bridges look like something from a fairy tale, with twisting and winding roots wrapping around each other.

In the midst of the monsoon season, the streams and running rivers fill up, making the riverbanks muddy and unsafe. Crossing the rivers and gorges can be extremely dangerous, so the locals have come up with a clever way of protecting the ecosystem while ensuring safe passage. Since *Ficus elastica* grows in abundance, the Khasi people take cuttings from mature trees, planting them on one side of the riverbank. Once the cutting has grown to maturity, its aerial roots, which are rope-like and easy to train, begin to emerge and are wound across bamboo or other deadwood structures. Once the fast-growing aerial roots are wound across to the other side, they are implanted into the soil of the opposing bank. There they quickly begin to thicken and a sturdy structure is formed. The bamboo supports break down, and the secondary growth of the roots and the formation of bark makes the bridge sturdy enough to cross. This process can take up to 15 years to complete, but many of the bridges can hold more than 50 people at once. They cost nothing to build and never weaken, only growing stronger with time. Some of the bridges are hundreds and hundreds of years old.

"These bridges are living, breathing examples of life in the past that can help us create sustainable lifestyles for the future."

—

Prasenjeet Yadav,
molecular biologist
and photographer

Depending on their function (whether the bridges are made to carry people or materials), the bridges vary massively in structure. Some have handrails for stability, while others have low sides. Some have a second layer, making them double-decker bridges. Some are wide and long, whereas others can only fit one person at a time. Once the bridges have thickened and are stable enough to cross, many of them are filled in at the base with mud, rocks, stones and boards to create a safe path to walk on.

This works well for the communities living in the Khasi Hills because there is no need to bring in materials like steel. Not only would this be costly, but also steel bridges would need repairing over time due to landslides and floods, and their construction would be very damaging to the sacred groves and wildlife. These bridges have been referred to in literature as 'living tree bridges in a land of clouds'. This simple statement perfectly honours the beauty of bio-engineering developed by the communities living here.

LATEX AS RUBBER

There are undeniably many uses for a *Ficus elastica*, but the common name 'rubber plant' gives a hint to one of the its main cultural and global uses. Although this common name can be misleading – *Ficus elastica* is often mistaken for *Hevea brasiliensis*, the plant responsible for the production of natural rubber throughout the world and a member of the Euphorbiaceae family (page 54). Both plants, when cut into, produce a milky-white sap known as latex, and this latex, when refined, is used to make rubber. Interestingly, the sap which bleeds from a dandelion has the exact same latex make-up as both *Hevea brasiliensis* and *Ficus elastica*. In theory, you could make rubber products from dandelions – providing you could harvest enough sap.

F. elastica was used historically as one of the main sources of rubber throughout the world, which is perhaps how the plant acquired its common name – but when compared to hevea, ficus is much less efficient at making enough rubber to keep up with modern global demands, and the tree takes much longer to recover between harvests. Although *H. brasiliensis* is responsible for 99 per cent of the world's natural rubber, *F. elastica* is still occasionally used, and both plants produce the same high-quality product.

The harvesting and manufacture of rubber is pretty simple. Rubber-producing trees are grown in groves in places like Malaysia and Thailand. The tree doesn't need to be cut down for its latex to be harvested, and so rubber groves are rarely expanded – making it a relatively environmentally friendly process. First, the rubber plants are 'tapped' by well-trained and experienced rubber tappers; this is done by making an incision in the bark and placing a cup below the incision to collect the latex. Then, ammonia is added so that the latex doesn't solidify as it's being harvested. Once this mixture is collected, an acid is added to refine and remove the liquid so that the rubber is properly extracted and there are no other components left from the latex. This process can take as long as 12 hours to complete and the resulting material looks a bit like sticky putty.

The refined rubber is then rolled through a machine to remove excess moisture and hung up on racks, either in specially made smokehouses or amid the groves, to dry. Once dry, the rubber looks a little like white leather. It's then stacked up and taken away to be processed into a usable product.

Records show that ficus latex was used in Central and South America – in paintings, rituals and medicine – as far back as 1600 BCE. Much later on, in the 17th century, a Mexican missionary spoke of indigenous and Spanish settlers in South America dipping their shoes and clothing into liquid latex to make them more durable and waterproof (like the first-ever pair of wellington boots). Nowadays, the latex is refined and components are added to ensure that the rubber is durable and doesn't break down in extreme temperatures – but the process of harvesting remains almost the same as it was in the 1600s.

Rubber is still used to this day to make all manner of things – tyres, shoes, gloves, surgical equipment, hot water bottles, pillows and mattresses, earphones and countless other everyday items many of us take for granted. Because global demand for rubber has risen exponentially, much of the rubber we come across in our daily lives is synthetic, but it is possible to scout out natural rubber when buying shoes and other items – and the real thing is much more durable, so well worth the slightly higher cost associated with it.

MORE THAN MEETS THE EYE

So, while *F. elastica* may not be the most exciting houseplant to look at – its value is held in its cultural ties and use throughout the world, not only in the production of rubber but also in its winding aerial roots and the living bridges that are made from them. Unfortunately, in cultivation, rubber plants rarely ever grow to be large enough for us to observe the true beauty of their aerial roots. If they do, there's not a whole lot that houseplant lovers can do with them. But maybe next time you see your rubber plant starting to unfurl a new leaf, you'll be reminded of the river-spanning structures that it has the potential to create.

Marimo Balls
(moss balls)

Native Locations
Iceland, Japan,
Ukraine, Australia,
Estonia and UK

"Kind treatment is necessary before mere protection."

—— **Misao Tatewaki,** botanist
On the preservation of
marimo

Marimo balls, also known as 'moss balls', have become increasingly popular among houseplant lovers keen to grow hassle-free aquatic plants with limited space. Their satisfyingly round shape, lush green colour and velvety texture have made them an image of intrigue and botanical interest throughout the Western plant market.

Marimo form in freshwater lakes in the northern hemisphere in a select few countries – mainly Iceland, Japan and Ukraine, but they can also be found in Australia, Estonia and the northern-most parts of Scotland. They require a rather particular set of conditions to grow, making them a rarity throughout the world: the lake must be ex-glacial, crystal clear and windy, allowing for choppy waters, which are essential in forming their characteristic shape.

While often sold under the name 'moss ball', these aquatic plants have no affiliation with moss at all and are in fact made up of densely packed algae aggregates (*Aegagropila linnaei*). While these species of algae are remarkably common, it is the spherical form they take on that is only possible under very particular conditions.

CHAPTER 4: IN CULTURE 99

The algae form around a small stone at the bottom of a lake. Over time, as the algae build up and become quite large, they break loose and begin to roll around the soft sedimented floor, being moulded and shaped into a sphere by wave motions in the lakes. This motion both moulds the shape of the marimo and stops any build-up of debris over time. Some marimo can grow to be as large as 30 cm (12 in) in diameter over the span of hundreds of years.

BOUNCY BALLS OF JAPAN

The word 'marimo' has been adopted by many Western countries from the Japanese name given to the algae balls. In Japanese, *mari* means 'bouncy ball' and *mo* means 'aquatic plant'. This name is testimony to how beloved marimo are in Japanese culture, which features plush toys and characters based on the bouncing aquatic novelty. Japanese families often keep marimo balls, passing them down to younger generations as an heirloom or keepsake.

There is even a legend, which accompanies the sacred value of the marimo, that goes as follows … Long ago, the daughter of a chief from a tribe living on Japan's Hokkaido island fell in love with a commoner and eloped. Her parents opposed the union, and so the couple ran away. But, tragically, they fell into Lake Akan and sunk to the bottom, where they were immortalised as marimo.

Hokkaido's Lake Akan is the only lake where marimo are grown, and the indigenous Ainu people have such admiration for their national treasure that they host an annual marimo festival, where people parade, dress up and dance in honour of the aquatic plant. During the three-day festivities, the elders teach kids about conservation, instilling the importance of keeping the lake clean to preserve the landscape's natural balance. Ainu people take marimo preservation very seriously, and drastic measures have been taken to reduce pollution on the island in an attempt to protect the plant.

ICELANDIC IDIOSYNCRASIES

Meanwhile in Iceland, these balls of algae have proven quite a nuisance to some. They are often referred to as *kúluskítur* ('muck ball' or 'shit ball') by fishermen, who bear the annoyance of dealing with marimo getting caught in the bottom of their fishing nets. Other locals love them and are more respectful, mercifully dubbing them 'lake balls' instead. Many Icelandic conservationists study the marimo and consider them an essential part of the ecosystem.

In 2014, disaster struck in Iceland. The number of marimo found in Lake Mývatn (which boasted the highest number in the country) dropped dramatically until there were none left. Local people grieved, worried that the sudden drop in number marked the onset of damaging changes to the surrounding ecosystem, comparing it to the death of a canary in a coal mine. Scientists put the loss down to air pollution caused by nearby mining. The build-up of pollution had increased the number of sun-blocking algae on the lake's surface. Without access to sunlight, the marimo stopped forming; and old marimo, some the size of volleyballs, were dragged underneath the surface of the sediment, where they suffocated.

Luckily, 2017 saw marimo numbers back on the rise. While the cause has not been established, the algae responsible for forming these velvety balls of joy in Lake Mývatn became more prevalent, and lower levels of the sun-blocking surface algae were reported. In 2018, the lake had another good year, and nearby residents reported seeing small marimo washing up on the shores – a sure sign that the natural balance was slowly being restored.

Although many houseplant shops, aquariums and novelty stores have taken advantage of the trend, the plants passed off as marimo are often just balls of moss. Real marimo are rare and should not be gathered for cultivation. While it's unlikely the marimo sold in stores are true marimo, they are nevertheless quite charming and represent a fascinating environmental and cultural wonder.

Terrariums

"Who loves a garden loves a greenhouse too."

—— William Cowper, poet

You would certainly be forgiven for thinking of terrariums as a very recent phenomenon, only becoming mainstream with the increased popularity of houseplants in recent years, but they have in fact been around for centuries, with sealed or wet terrariums being used for both decorative and practical purposes as far back as the 1800s. Although open or dry terrariums are relatively new to the scene in comparison, and don't have quite the same historical uses, they are still beneficial to the plants growing within, just like their sealed counterparts.

GARDENING IN MINIATURE

First up, we should probably explain the difference between the two. Open (sometimes known as dry or desert) terrariums usually come in the form of a geometric or glasshouse-style vessel with a pane or two of glass missing, or in vase-like form with an open top (although the lack of drainage here can be problematic). This style of terrarium is best for housing desert or succulent plants because open terrariums don't retain moisture or humidity. They also amplify light levels, which, although not ideal for tropical plants, is just what desert dwellers need. Another benefit to housing your succulents and cacti in open terrariums is that it can help to protect them from unfavourable environments in the home that could potentially harm their growth, such as extended periods of cold, increased humidity levels, or strong draughts, while simultaneously creating a microclimate that mimics that of their natural habitat.

CHAPTER 4: IN CULTURE 103

Sealed terrariums are a little more complex in nature but essentially do the same job of protecting the plants within from harsh external environments – this time by housing tropical and subtropical plants, or any plants that prefer a damp and dark environment, and shielding them from harmful dry air while minimising the chances of underwatering. In theory, housing moisture-loving plants in a sealed terrarium should make them much easier to care for and dramatically decrease the amount of attention you need to give them (although we have found we pay them much more notice once planted in a terrarium because the changes you'll see are fascinating!). Kept in the right conditions, you should only need to water your terrarium after months – sometimes you won't need to water them at all!

The reason for this is because the plants, mosses and minerals in your sealed terrarium should have created their own microclimate where they can interact and live as they would in their natural habitats, thriving off each other and using what's around them for sustenance. Because the bottle is sealed and moisture cannot escape, your terrarium should be self-sustaining. It should have been watered when it was first made, and that water should have stayed inside the terrarium. Water is given in mist form and fills the air inside the vessel with moisture. It then falls to the soil below, providing water for the plants' roots. The roots absorb it and feed it up to the leaves, which transpire during photosynthesis, releasing water back into the air and starting the cycle again. There will likely be a time when you will have to water a terrarium again because not all the water that plants take up is released back into the air; but we highly doubt you'll mind when the time comes, as by then you will have saved yourself hundreds of trips to the sink.

NATHANIEL BAGSHAW
AND HIS WARDIAN CASE

The beneficial effects of growing plants in sealed glass vessels were first discovered in 1829 in London by a medical professional with a passionate interest in botany and entomology: Nathaniel

Bagshaw Ward. At the time of the discovery, Ward was observing the behaviours and evolution of a moth, whose chrysalis he had placed onto a bed of compost in a glass jar, in order to study it. In the unattended jar, a fern spore grew and germinated into a fully fledged fern, resulting in the first terrarium. This came to be known as a Wardian case. Ward set up more of these sealed environments and filled them with plants he had struggled to keep alive in the past, due to the inhospitable London environment. To his surprise, he found the plants thrived in ways he could never have imagined. He realised that the plants released oxygen as they photosynthesised, which would condense on the glass and drip down to the roots. With this discovery, his Wardian cases became of great interest to botanists and explorers, who were travelling the world by ship and wanted to bring their plant discoveries home.

Surprisingly, up until this point, there was only about a 2 per cent survival rate on plants being transported between countries, with species often dying because of the less-than-ideal conditions on board a ship. Above deck, tropical species were often faced with prolonged periods of harsh sunlight and would suffer a battering from the strong winds. Below deck, it was sweltering in the warmer climates and freezing in the cooler, never mind the fact the plants were being watered with salty water from the sea!

Ward alerted fellow botanical enthusiast and friend (and, at the time, director of the Chelsea Physic Garden) Robert Fortune to his discovery, and they hired a group of carpenters to build a great range of Wardian cases to aid in exporting British plants to Sydney, Australia. When the plants arrived in great condition after months of travel across the previously treacherous seas, they sent plants from abroad back to London using the same cases. Again, the plants arrived in perfect condition. This was the start of the mass moving of plants around the world, with Wardian cases being used for decades by great botanical establishments such as Kew, and esteemed botanists and botanical societies, to bring in exotic plants from across the British Empire. Unbelievably, the success rate grew from the diabolical 2 per cent to over 80 per cent with the introduction of the cases – a world-changing discovery indeed.

POPULARITY – THEN AND NOW

Unsurprisingly, with the successful transportation of tropical plants to the UK came their soaring popularity among the general population. Tropical plants, especially those kept in Wardian cases at home, became a sort of status symbol and sign of wealth between the upper classes. Bigger and better cases were being created all the time, and the sealed containers ensured the survival of these delicate plants without the need for a full-on greenhouse or much in the way of care. Being in possession of such exotic plants that had only just been introduced to the country must have felt very special indeed. Ferns and palms became particularly popular (both plants that do very well inside terrariums, as I'm sure you gauged by the fact that ferns are what led to the discovery) during the Victorian era and you will notice that interiors – from wallpapers to soft furnishings – from that time are often adorned with tropical-looking leaves. Tropical palm houses went up in many of the country's botanical gardens and the trend known as pteridomania (obsession with anything to do with ferns) continued to grow.

By contrast, terrariums today are not so much of a status symbol and sign of wealth, but more a way of getting our green-fingered fix with the limited outdoor space most city dwellers are subject to. They're an indoor extension of gardening, providing all the same benefits but on a smaller scale. Although we have a better understanding now of what our tropical plants need in order to survive (never mind better heating and insulation in our homes), it can still be tricky in certain homes to keep them, and terrariums are still the best solution to that problem. Somewhere between their original discovery and now (probably the houseplant mania of the 1970s), the shape evolved from that of the original Wardian case (think miniature greenhouse) to the bottle-style terrariums we most commonly see today, and the array of objects used as terrariums grows on an almost monthly basis. Anything you can make airtight can be used. More intricate methods of filling them have been developed because of the bottles with particularly narrow necks, and so the satisfaction that comes with the precision when making one has become a hobby in itself.

CLOSING THE CASE

Whether it's the joy of creating your own miniature garden (and actually making it *inside* a glass bottle), the delights of watching one evolve in your home or the joy of finally being able to keep tropical plants in a space with dry air, there are plenty of reasons to have a terrarium of your own. Watching the life cycles of each plant, seeing how the stronger species will start to dominate, watching others die off and biodegrading to feed the survivors before sprouting again from the still active root base – all of this natural wonder is easily observed when you own a terrarium. As a result, you'll have a much deeper understanding of the natural ecosystems that occur in the wild, so you can add 'learning experience' to the list of reasons you should get one.

CHAPTER 5

INTERESTING ADAPTATIONS

Mimosa Pudica
(the sensitive plant)

Native Locations
South and
Central America

> "*Brains and neurones are a sophisticated solution,
> but not a necessary requirement for learning.*"
>
> —— Monica Gagliano, biologist

Mimosa pudica, more commonly called 'the sensitive plant', is famous for its bashful behaviour, cringing its leaves and stems away from even the slightest of stimuli. In fact, the Latin *pudica* literally translates to 'bashful' or 'shy'.

For those unfamiliar with the plant, *M. pudica* could be likened to a mix between a Venus flytrap, with its sudden, dramatic movements and a delicate fern – much like maidenhair.

MIMOSA IN THE WILD

They begin life as small, upright plants, but as they mature, they lie low to the ground in a sprawling fashion, with stems often reaching 1.5 metres (5 feet). Their timid foliage resembles that of a fern, with small compound leaves. They display extremely defensive behaviour, with both the folding away of their leaves to ward off insects, pests and predators, and a prickly petiole (the stalk that attaches the leaf of a plant to the stem) to disarm those who dare to chance a nibble.

M. pudica is native to South and Central America but has been introduced to many other tropical and subtropical climates around the world. They're most commonly regarded as an invasive weed and can be found growing near shady walls, by the side of the road or in any other busy environment where their need for warm, humid air, water and shade is catered to.

BOTANICAL CURIOSITY

As with many other botanical curiosities, these plants gained notoriety in the world of horticulture by displaying, within their leaf movements, a unique quality that many of us hadn't seen before. This is most likely because *M. pudica* are very difficult to grow outside of their natural environment unless you can recreate the conditions they find most habitable. So it wasn't really until the houseplant trend took off that many of us were exposed to, and able to cultivate, so many new varieties of these intriguing tropical plants. All the while, biologists and botanists have grown mimosa for hundreds of years. They use them to study plant behaviours, such as light response and plant memory. Yes, you read that right.

But surely plants can't remember? If you factor their lack of a brain into the equation. Well, actually, thanks to the noble mimosa and the botanists who have studied them, we're beginning to understand plant memory in greater depth than ever before.

Studies carried out in the 1960s came to prove that *M. pudica* could differentiate between stimuli. For example, it could tell the difference between the brush of a finger (which would cause the leaves to close up) and a drop of water falling on the leaves (after which the leaves wouldn't move). This comes in handy for the mimosa in the wild, especially in the wet season. It would need a lot of energy if it had to close its leaves every time it was hit by a raindrop, rendering the species extinct pretty quickly.

MIMOSA AND MEMORY

In 2014, Monica Gagliano, a biologist, performed an experiment in which she dropped mimosa in pots from a height of 15 cm (6 in). She observed that the plants would close their leaves in an act of protection against the unknown stimulus. She then repeated this experiment every 5 seconds for 5 minutes until the mimosa came to realise that the stimulus wasn't harmful, and that closing its leaves was a waste of precious energy. Instead, the plants kept their leaves open when they were dropped.

One week later, Gagliano repeated her experiment, dropping the plants from the same height as before. Incredibly, the leaves remained open. The same was true when she performed the experiment a few months later. Could this mean the plant remembered the stimulus wasn't harmful? Could it retain the memory for longer?

Some sceptics doubted this was the case and said the plants were just exhausted and unable to muster the energy necessary to close their leaves. Gagliano was prepared for this, however. She then introduced a new stimulus (shaking the plant), which could have been harmful for the mimosa. The leaves immediately closed up, just as they had at the beginning of the experiment, disproving this theory in a matter of minutes, and seeming to prove that plants are capable of storing information in the form of 'memories'.

PLANT INTELLIGENCE

With new discoveries and advancements in technology every day, our minds become increasingly open to the potential of the natural world; and yet it seems the more we learn, the more we realise that we have only scratched the surface of what plants are capable of.

Whether or not you believe that plants have the capacity for memory and 'intelligence', Gagliano's study brings light to a topic seemingly plucked from sci-fi. Without need for an award or praise, at the very least much credit is due to the invaluable, bashful mimosa.

Echeveria

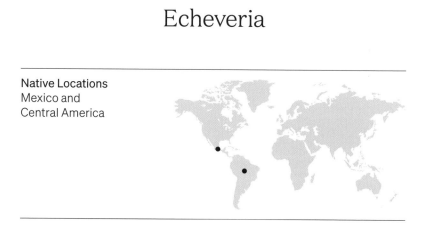

Native Locations
Mexico and
Central America

"A rose in the desert can only survive on its strength, not its beauty."

—— Matshona Dhliwayo, writer

Echeveria are perhaps the most well-known of all succulents within the houseplant world. They are popular for their rosette-forming leaves, vast array of cultivars and varieties, and their ease of growing and propagation. It's common to see the leaves of an echeveria placed in a circle on a pot on the soil propagating themselves on social media posts and in gardening magazines. While the sweet succulent has gained a lot of notoriety in social media and in popular culture, there is a whole other life going on in the background that most of us are unaware of, with interesting adaptations helping them to survive the harsh landscapes they are found growing in naturally.

SOAKING UP THE SUN

Echeveria grow naturally in an array of arid conditions across the globe. The genus has such a multitude of varieties and cultivars, it can be difficult to trace their lineage back to one point; but it is generally thought that they are native to Central and South America, and the diverse set of adaptations they display are a

testament to their native habitat. They are often found basking in hot full-sun conditions, seemingly unaware of the scorching UV rays (or perhaps just enjoying them).

Growing in sandy, free-draining soil, echeveria thrive in pretty much any spot where their love of the sun is catered to. This could be in the middle of an open, barren desert; on the roadside; growing from nooks and crannies in walls and stonework; or even creeping their way into someone's back garden. Wherever the plant is found, they seem to enjoy being on, around or near to rocks, boulders and stones the best, absorbing second-hand heat or sheltering themselves from drying winds. Because vegetative propagation (breeding from an aerial part of the plant) is so easy for an echeveria, they can often be observed growing in small communities, surrounded by other echeveria and succulents from genera such as *Sedum*, *Sempervivum* and *Kalanchoe*.

The plants themselves do not need a lot of growing room and seem perfectly happy squeezing into tight spots between stones where they can bask in warmth and full sun. Their shallow, far-reaching roots (a common adaptation in many xerophytes), allow them to harvest any available water from the surface of the soil; and so when there are huge communities of echeveria growing together, their roots as a whole make a sort of water-catching net. Perhaps this is why they seem so confident and content to bathe in the sun, seemingly free from worries of water loss and sunscorch.

VARIETIES AND ADAPTATIONS

Echeveria, as a genus, has utilised a number of different adaptations to ensure their success in the wild. These adaptations have affected many aspects of the plant's physical appearance, and so there are a great deal of varieties and cultivars available, all with a functional and interesting backstory.

As we mentioned earlier, these plants have no problem propagating themselves, both vegetatively and by seed. And since they often grow en masse in huge communities, a lot of natural variations have arisen over the years. With natural variations being difficult to trace, and with humans harvesting and cultivating new types of echeveria all the time, most resulting echeveria lose their species names and are instead simply given cultivar names, without any indication as to where the plants have originated or who their close family members might be. Another example of a plant whose species names have either been lost, are untraceable, or are too complex to be shared by plant breeders with the general public, is roses, which are regularly referred to simply by their given cultivar name. (See page 16 to read about the difference between cultivars, varieties and hybrids.)

Since there are so many varieties and cultivars of echeveria, it can be hard to say whether unique characteristics are a result of exaggerated man-made breeding or of environmental necessity. Breeders will single out plants with singular qualities (often resulting from necessary adaptations) and breed them with other plants to create new hybrids and cultivars for the plant market. For example, the red colouring on the leaves of many species of echeveria (page 114) is an adaptation the plant has evolved as a way to survive periods of extreme, intense sun. To a plant breeder, these red tips are an attractive visual add-on, and so they have bred the red-tipped echeveria species with *Echeveria agavoides* to create the now well-known cultivar *Echeveria agavoides* 'Red Tip'.

We discuss a few of the more unusual succulent adaptations in our section on Senecio rowleyanus (page 122), but there are some fundamental adaptations which apply to a myriad of succulents that we haven't covered, and echeveria are host to many such adaptations.

HAIRY LEAVES:
ECHEVERIA 'DORIS TAYLOR'

The hairs on the leaves of a plant, known botanically as 'trichomes', serve an array of different purposes depending on the plant and the environment surrounding it. A plant's trichomes can be long and thick, or small and subtle – they are as diverse and multifunctional as human hairs. For some plants, hairy leaves serve the purpose of trapping humidity, while in others they help to regulate temperature. Some plants use trichomes to ward off pests, which have difficulty climbing among the bristles.

In *Echeveria* 'Doris Taylor', and other hairy-leaved succulents, however, the trichomes serve a dual purpose. First, pale-coloured or white trichomes are used to reflect the harshest and most damaging UV-A and UV-B rays. In this instance, the plant doesn't usually have another barrier like the powdery leaves mentioned below or the thick waxy cuticle mentioned above. However, some studies have suggested that a fine coating of trichomes is actually more effective at protecting plants from UV rays than a waxy cuticle.

The second reason that plants like *E*. 'Doris Taylor' produce their characteristic hairy leaves is down to the conservation of water. The trichomes help to create a barrier between the leaves and the atmosphere surrounding them, so when transpiration occurs, the water becomes trapped in the trichomes and water loss is minimal. This also creates a small area of humidity around the leaves, meaning that the temperature is slightly lower, which in turn reduces the chance of transpiration. The trichomes also guide water to the roots of the plant – so when it rains, the water becomes trapped in the hairs and the droplets run straight down to the roots, which absorb the water to be stored in the plant's succulent leaves.

POWDERY LEAVES: ECHEVERIA SUBSESSILIS

The powder on the leaves of a plant, like the powdery 'bloom' found on the surface of a grape, is known botanically as 'epicuticular wax', and is so named because it forms on top of the cuticle (secreted by the epidermis) we mentioned earlier. This waxy coating, once again, can perform a variety of different roles, depending on where it is found. The bloom on a grape, for example, is secreted in order to protect the fruit from pests, who find the bloom too slippery to land and crawl around on. Less specifically, the function of this epicuticular wax is to form a kind of protective shield, or barrier, over whatever it happens to be sitting atop.

In the case of *E. subsessilis* and many other varieties and cultivars of echeveria, as well as a number of other succulents, epicuticular wax serves two primary functions. The first is, once again, a way to help the plant deal with extreme UV rays. By secreting the bloom, succulents create a sort of natural suncream for themselves. Since the bloom is a whitish colour, it reflects the harshest of UV rays, and stops the plant from being overexposed to the worst of the sun. This is similar to the way someone cultivating plants in a greenhouse might paint the glass roof chalky white to stop plants from burning in the summer. As a general rule, the more sunlight a plant with epicuticular wax is exposed to, the more wax it secretes to protect itself.

The second fundamental function also ties in with why an echeveria might produce extra-thick, waxy cuticles on their leaves – to create a barrier between the leaves and the atmosphere surrounding them. By secreting this wax on the surface of their leaves, the plant is able to lock moisture in and protects itself from too much evapotranspiration (transpiration via evaporation). This would work in a similar way to if you or I wore light clothing that cover our whole bodies while holidaying in a desert climate.

As with the waxy bloom coating of a grape, epicuticular wax also serves to help protect echeveria from pests. The slippery coating makes gripping on to the leaves near impossible and the laying of eggs even harder. Any carefully laid eggs are likely to slip off, which renders the whole process a waste of precious energy for any pest.

RED AND DARK PURPLE LEAVES:
ECHEVERIA 'BLACK PRINCE'

We chose *Echeveria* 'Black Prince' because it is perhaps the most obvious cultivar to display a deep reddish-purple colour; however, a great number of other echeverias will become red or purple at the tips or all the way through the leaves as a response to environmental factors.

First, it may help to understand why a plant's leaves change colour, and which pigments are behind the phenomenon. Chlorophyll is the pigment found in plants and algae, and produces the characteristic green colour that we associate with plant life; chlorophyll is an essential component in photosynthesis and allows plants to harvest sunlight to produce energy. In most plants, there are a number of different pigments that work together to achieve the same end, but chlorophyll is usually the most dominant, which is why, in optimal conditions, plants appear green to us.

Chlorophyll is, however, one of the more sensitive pigments within a plant, and it doesn't do well in extreme temperatures or in extreme sun. When the weather becomes very hot and sunny or very cold, the production of chlorophyll drops, the chlorophyll begins to die, and other pigments within the leaf take over the job of harvesting light for the plant. The pigments that pick up most of the slack are carotenoids – which, as their name might suggest, are responsible for giving orange carrots (as opposed to purple varieties) and other yellow or orange fruits and vegetables (such as tangerines and bananas) their colour – and anthocyanins, which are responsible for deep reds, purples and blues within the plant world (such as in plums, blueberries and cherries).

Since chlorophyll production is hindered in extreme conditions, and any existing chlorophyll is likely to die off (without secondary help – in other words, waxy cuticles or hairy leaves), plants living in very hot or very cold temperatures tend to be more red or purple in colour, whereas plants living in temperate or tropical climates, unexposed to extreme temperatures, tend to be more lush and green in colour. This phenomenon, known as chlorophyll degradation, is also the reason that leaves on deciduous trees (those that drop their leaves before turning dormant in the winter) turn yellow, red or purple before falling off in the autumn.

So when it comes to echeveria, and some other succulent plants, the changing of colour from green to red during hot, sunny weather is not abnormal. It simply means that less chlorophyll is being produced (or that the chlorophyll is dying), and anthocyanins are taking over. While some may mistake this for sunburn (which can also happen!), it is a perfectly natural phenomenon and a great adaptation to help sun-dwelling plants to deal with extreme temperature and harsh UV rays in the wild.

ADAPTATIONS TO ADMIRE

Echeveria, it seems, have been one of the most popular genera of succulent for a very long time. With so many different types out there, and with so many of us growing them at home, it's not hard to appreciate them for their myriad of colours, shapes and sizes. Hopefully we can start to gain a new-found level of appreciation for all of the diverse adaptations these rose-like succulents have evolved. And perhaps when you next look at your succulent collection, you'll be able to see deeper into their history and admire them not just for their outward appearance but also for their inner workings.

Senecio Rowleyanus

(string of pearls)

Native Location
Little Karoo in
South Africa

*"Look closely at nature. Every species is a masterpiece,
exquisitely adapted to the particular environment
in which it has survived."*

—— E.O. Wilson, biologist and writer

Senecio rowleyanus, more commonly known as 'string of pearls', is a houseplant that has risen dramatically in popularity in the last five years or so, due to its presence on social media and in interior design magazines. Its trailing stems and pearl-like leaves, which inspired its nickname, bring forth an image of elegance. Their round shape and mossy-green colour are satisfying to the eye and are vaguely reminiscent of the beloved marimo (page 98). Although string of pearls looks as though it belongs in a Japanese moss garden, the genus the plant comes from, *Senecio*, is a rather prominent member of the Asteraceae family (also known as the daisy family), which boasts a significant number of popular and well-known outdoor plants, including sunflowers, dahlias, common daisies and chamomile plants.

Plants within the *Senecio* genus are distributed throughout the world and include *Senecio vulgaris*, or 'groundsel', which has pom-pom-shaped seed heads similar to a dandelion. While it may be hard to believe that this beloved houseplant belongs to the same

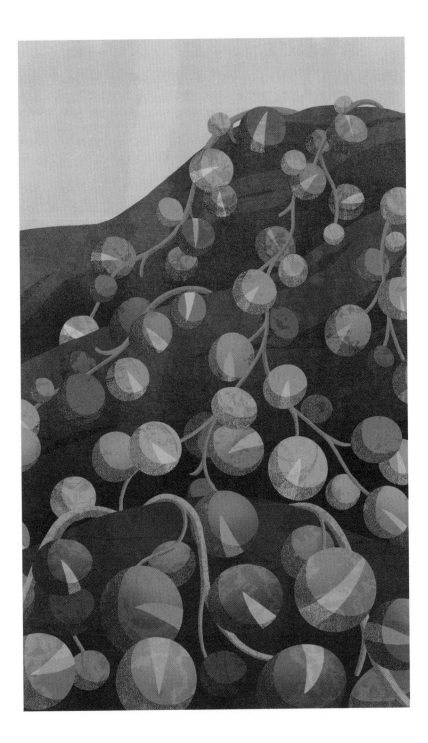

genus as a British garden weed, their tell-tale, clove-scented flowers are characteristic of all members.

WHERE AND HOW THEY GROW

Senecio rowleyanus is a succulent (water-storing) member of the genus, among many, which are native to South Africa. They grow in the wilderness in arid, desert-like conditions where there is very little rainfall – and full, hot sun and dry winds are the norms. Although they come from a highly unfavourable climate, and weather conditions are harsh, a string of pearls can often be found shying away from the extremes around rocks and boulders or growing in the shade and shelter provided by bigger plants and trees.

Although we tend to regard string of pearls as hanging or trailing plants, they actually grow in their native habitat as scrambling vines, forming dense mats on the ground or over rocks. The plants themselves can extend their trailing stems to be as long as 1 metre (3 feet), and sometimes even longer. Their stems bear tiny, almost imperceptible roots, which help them to scramble along the ground, anchoring themselves for stability as they go. These roots are known as adventitious roots and make self-propagation easy; they also mean that the plant doesn't have to expend too much energy reproducing by seed during the hottest and driest months.

ADAPTATIONS FOR SURVIVAL

Life in such an unforgiving landscape can cause problems for any unprepared, or rather, unevolved plant, and so, as with many others growing in the desert, string of pearls have developed a number of adaptations over time in order to maximise their chances of survival. Most of these can be observed in other species growing in the same landscape, which serves as a testimony to their usefulness.

Although many desert plants evolve for the purpose of handling heat and UV rays, most changes are formed as a way to cope with the lack of water provided in deserts and other hot, dry climates. Plants that have evolved with adaptations to help them survive with rare and irregular water supplies are commonly called 'xerophytes' – a term which refers to most, if not all, desert plants, including all succulents and cacti.

The following adaptations aren't unique to string of pearls, but the combination of all of the following is perhaps what make this humble houseplant so tenacious and admirable.

Reduced leaves

Reduced leaves are a common adaptation found in a number of xerophytes, as well as alpine plants that live on dry, sunny mountainsides, plants living within the Arctic Circle, and a great number of others found in climates that are dry or have extreme temperatures. Cacti are a prime example of reduced leaves; in fact, their leaves are so heavily reduced that they have turned into the infamous spines we all associate with cacti today. Most xerophytes use reduced leaves as a way of conserving water and reducing UV damage in hot, dry conditions. The leaves of a string of pearls are not only heavily reduced, but are also succulent, giving them double the advantage in their habitat. But what's the benefit of having such small leaves? And does this disadvantage the plant when it comes to photosynthesis?

The leaves of all plants contain stomata (breathing pores) on the underside. These stomata are invisible to the naked eye but can be seen underneath a microscope. The stomata open and close to exchange gases with the air (carbon dioxide and oxygen); when the stomata are open, water is lost through the leaf through transpiration – the plant equivalent of sweating.

Plants with large leaves have more stomata and are therefore more likely to lose water to the atmosphere – which is fine for those living in tropical and subtropical climates, where humidity is high and water is readily available (this is why many plants from the tropics have large leaves). But having large leaves would be extremely problematic to plants living in arid climates. If large leaves have more stomata, it then stands to reason that plants with smaller leaves have fewer stomata to worry about; the fewer of these there are, the less likely a plant is to lose water via transpiration to the surrounding atmosphere.

Having large leaves in the desert would very quickly prove fatal to a plant: in a day or two, the leaves would dehydrate, wilt, and the plant would die. By having small leaves, a string of pearls has fewer stomata, and so the rate of transpiration is greatly reduced, and the plant doesn't dehydrate as quickly in the hot weather in South Africa.

CAM photosynthesis

Crassulacean acid metabolism, or CAM for short, is an adaptation that was first discovered in the Crassulaceae family, which is where the name comes from. CAM is an adaptation that many xerophytes use to further conserve water in hot, dry weather and it once again involves the stomata (breathing pores) mentioned earlier.

In plants living in more favourable climates, photosynthesis takes on a normal course: plants absorb sunlight during the day and open their stomata to exchange essential gases with the air. Since plants need carbon dioxide from their environment to photosynthesise, having the stomata open enables both this and the release of oxygen, a natural by-product of photosynthesis, to the surrounding atmosphere.

However, as we previously mentioned, a desert plant having its stomata open during the day could mean that a fatal amount of water would be lost, and it would quickly become dehydrated in the desert heat; and so plants like string of pearls have found a different way to photosynthesise. Rather than having their stomata open during the day and losing all of their specially conserved water, many desert plants instead simply keep their stomata closed. They still absorb sunlight during the day as other plants do, but save their gaseous exchange for when the temperature has dropped enough to safely open their stomata. And so, during the night, when the temperature has dropped, the stomata open and exchange gases with the surrounding atmosphere. But without sunlight, photosynthesis cannot take place – so plants that practise CAM photosynthesis absorb carbon dioxide from the surrounding atmosphere and change its composition, storing it within their cells until the sun returns. When that happens, the stomata close back up and the plant harvests sunlight, simultaneously changing the carbon dioxide within the plant back to its original composition and using it to complete photosynthesis. To avoid opening its stomata, the plant stores the oxygen (a by-product of the process) within its cells – so when the sun leaves once again, the stomata can reopen and the oxygen is released.

There is a well-known myth that has circulated for years which suggests that keeping plants in your bedroom is bad for your health – but this process not only dispels the myth, but suggests the opposite is true. Many people keep succulents and cacti by their bedside as the release of oxygen during the night is, in fact, considered beneficial to a good night's sleep.

Epidermal windows

S. rowleyanus's small, pearl-shaped leaves are succulent and embellished with a see-through slit, like a crescent moon, that runs down the margin of the leaf. This is perhaps one of the most fascinating, and relatively rare, adaptations that this plant (and a few other xerophytes) exhibit. In botany, this translucent area is known as an 'epidermal window', although some call it a 'leaf window' – and this name reflects both the visual and physiological aspects of this adaptation.

Epidermal windows are found almost exclusively in succulents and are an adaptation to help the plant photosynthesise efficiently. Made up of layers of the epidermis (outer-most layer of the leaf), and several layers of parenchyma (inner tissues which also act as water storage), the window allows sunlight to penetrate the leaf and be directly absorbed by chlorophyll with no barriers in the way, maximising the rate of photosynthesis.

This adaptation is most commonly seen in succulent plants with a heavily reduced leaf surface area that would struggle to photosynthesise without it. This means that plants like string of pearls can have very small leaves, further reducing the risk of transpiration, while maximising sun uptake through their 'windows'.

Some plants, such as Lithops sp., also known as 'living stone' plants, grow in the same area in South Africa as string of pearls. They use epidermal windows on the top of their succulent leaves to photosynthesise while the rest of their leaves are buried underground in the hottest, driest weather, much like a frog peeking its beady eyes out of the water in a pond. By only exposing its epidermal windows, it can continue to photosynthesise without worrying about losing too much water to the heat.

TYING THE ADAPTATIONS TOGETHER

While each of the adaptations listed are extremely beneficial to any xerophyte, perhaps what makes string of pearls so successful is the fact that it uses all three listed adaptations together to maximise its chances of survival. With its small leaves, which reduce the number of stomata and therefore transpiration, paired with CAM photosynthesis, which further reduces the rate of transpiration during the day, and its epidermal windows, which mean that sunlight can penetrate every bit of chlorophyll in the leaf with no barriers – there is no way that a plant could be better adapted to suit its climate and to endure such an inhospitable environment. So what does this mean when it comes to growing the plants at home?

TAKE PRIDE IN YOUR PEARLS

In the shop, our customers often ask us what the best way to keep string of pearls alive is. It seems that many struggle to keep them, and so the best answer we can give is to try and understand the conditions of their natural habitat. All of the adaptations we have listed here refer to the fact that the plants live, grow and thrive in a hot, dry, sunny climate – and so we must treat them accordingly at home.

First, we can gather that they're not well adapted to dealing with the cold, so they should, ideally, be positioned somewhere warm, or at least somewhere with no cold draught or air conditioning nearby. Oddly enough – and this does go against all houseplant cultivation rules – we've found that a great deal of success in cultivating a string of pearls can come from having them positioned on, or near to, a radiator in the winter months. Next, the plants need light, and lots of it, so a bright, sunny room is the best spot for your pearly companion. Third, and perhaps less predictably, it's important to keep in mind that string of pearls grows as groundcover in the wild. It's no good keeping them on a high shelf. They need sun from the top down (so you're more likely to have success on a windowsill than a shelf).

Finally, these plants come from the desert – and one of the main characteristics of a desert is that it experiences irregular and infrequent rainfall. Overwatering your plant is a mistake we've all made in the past, but is one sure way to kill string of pearls; they don't like to have soggy feet. The best way to tell if your string of pearls needs a water is to look at the pearls. If they have 'deflated' a little, they are no longer full of water and would benefit from watering. If the pearls are still full, they're likely well hydrated and don't need watering – even if the soil is dry.

If you follow these tips (you can even apply them to other houseplants) you are sure to have success in keeping string of pearls alive at home. And when you do, you might well be able to spot the awesome adaptations this plant has evolved.

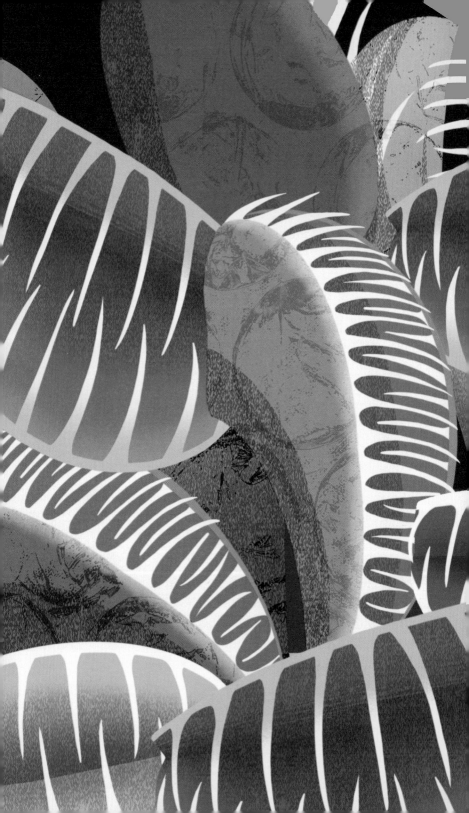

CHAPTER 6

CARNIVORES

Drosera

Drosera is a genus of 'flypaper' carnivorous plant (plants that use sticky mucous to trap insects), commonly referred to as sundews. The plant's common and Latin names were carefully selected and relate to their habit of growth and physiology. *Drosera* in Greek means 'dewy' and refers to the dewy secretions found on the ends of the tentacles which cover the leaves. The common name comes from an observation made by Henry Lyte, a botanist studying the plant in the 16th century (before Darwin discovered that the plants were carnivorous). While Lyte was working with *Drosera*, he found that the tentacles secreted more of the 'dew' when growing in sunnier conditions – thus, the plant was nicknamed the 'sundew'.

The genus *Drosera* is diverse, with around 200 known species found scattered across the globe. Species of sundew have been found in Alaska, Australia, the Bahamas, England and Siberia (among many others). The only continent without a habitat that supports a sundew's growth is Antarctica. As with most other carnivores, sundews can be found growing in boggy, nutrient-deficient, acidic soils, which is how the necessity for carnivory evolved. Depending on where the sundew comes from, leaves can be long and strap-like or wide and spoon-shaped. Their colouring varies from light green to dark red, and most sundews grow in a rosette, with the crown of the plant based close to the ground.

Although the sundew may seem the prettiest and meekest of all the carnivores, they are perhaps the most aggressive, trapping and digesting their prey in a way that would be blood-curdling, if not for their relatively small size.

DARWIN'S FASCINATION

Charles Darwin's name is familiar to most of us. When we hear it, perhaps the first thing that comes to mind is evolution. But Darwin had a great fascination for many different aspects of the natural world. Regarding plants, he studied their movement, gravitational force, light responses, their habit of growth, how they are fertilised and by which pollinators, among many other topics. But one topic always stood out to us as houseplant growers: carnivorous plants or, as Darwin called them, insectivorous plants.

Darwin studied carnivorous plants for decades. And through countless tests and experiments, he discovered new and exciting traits, along with a great deal of what we know today about how the plants trap, digest, absorb and differentiate between prey. But to Darwin, there was one plant genus that stood out and became more beloved to him than any of the others: *Drosera*. And when he finally published his works and findings in the book *Insectivorous Plants*, this was apparent. Out of 18 chapters in the book, 12 were focused on the sundews.

Although Darwin had come across the sundews before, while experimenting with the movement in plants, he took the time to study every aspect of their carnivory, such as how they responded to organic matter (beyond the insects he found in their tentacles), using bits of meat, cheese, chalk, leaves, glass and even some strands of his wife's hair. He also tested liquids such as water, milk and urine. By the end of his experimentation, he had tested more than 100 different organic and inorganic substances and had discovered that the sundews were capable of detecting nitrogen itself, which was scarce in the soil they grew in.

He also studied the movement of their tentacles, and how

"I have been infinitely amused by working at *Drosera*: the movements are really curious; and the manner in which the leaves detect certain nitrogenous compounds is marvellous."

—

Charles Darwin, naturalist, in a letter to American botanist Asa Gray, 26th September 1860 the plants trapped their prey into an immovable state. He looked at their triggering mechanisms, how the plants digest and reabsorb the nutrients from their prey and how this effected subsequent growth. And finally, he explored why the plants were carnivorous at all. He also drew the sundews regularly and kept his own personal sundews outside of his experimentation.

Having spent so much time studying one single plant and its responses, it comes as no surprise he felt so dearly about them. While performing his experiments, Darwin wrote a letter to a geologist friend, proudly proclaiming, 'At this moment I care more about *Drosera* than the origin of all the species in the world,' a rather resolute statement coming from the father of evolution. In another letter, he refers to *Insectivorous Plants* as 'my book on *Drosera* & co'. Finally, in a letter to American botanist Asa Gray, Darwin wrote, 'It is a wonderful plant, or rather a most sagacious animal. I will stick up for *Drosera* to the day of my death.' And he certainly did, passing his love for the sundews on to us and countless others.

TRAPPING MECHANISMS

Drosera is a large genus of plants distributed throughout the world, and as such, their growth can take on many different habits, shapes and sizes, depending on where the plants are found. Some are very small, and their leaves form rosettes close to the ground, while others, like *Drosera gigantea*, are tall and branching, with a shrub-like habit. The leaves can be small and round like a coin; some may be long and branching like a sort-of carnivorous tree, while others are long and strap-like. Some can be a mixture of both and branch out before becoming rounded, like a rosette of miniature wooden spoons. For all of their differences, one thing the sundews do have in common are the 'tentacles' that cover the tops of their leaves.

These 'tentacles' are stalked glands, which secrete sticky, dewy mucous at their tips. In most species of drosera, two different types of glands can be found, with two different functions. Stalked glands are found at the end of tentacles, and they serve the purpose of attracting and trapping prey before secreting digestive enzymes to break the prey down and harvest their nutrients. The second type of gland is a sessile gland, which sits in the centre of the leaf. The function of a sessile gland is to absorb the nutrients from the dead prey for use within the plant.

In some species, namely *D. glanduligera*, another type, known as a retentive gland, can be observed on the leaf's outer margins. This gland does not produce sticky mucous, as the stalked glands do, but instead serves to secure strong-willed or particularly large prey. These glands can move at an incredible speed, similar to a Venus flytrap or even the bashful mimosa (page 110). If the insect looks as though it might escape from the side of the leaf, the retentive glands curl over or use a snapping motion to push the unfortunate prey into the digestive stalked glands. There they become well and truly stuck, and any chance of escape becomes hopeless.

The prey of a sundew depends on where it is found growing, but usually their diet is restricted to small flying bugs and insects that are easy to trap and envelop. The carcasses of mosquitos, gnats, fruit flies, common flies, craneflies and ants are all commonly found stuck to smaller species of the plant. Occasionally, larger species of sundews will lure and trap more sizeable insects, such as dragonflies, wasps, spiders and moths.

The insects and beetles are lured into the sundew either by droplets of glistening mucilage on the tips of the tentacles that they mistake for nectar or, as Darwin suggested, odour emitted by the plant, which is unnoticeable to humans but very attractive to the insects. Darwin was never able to confirm this, but his theory was later proven to be true by Ashraf El-Sayed, a chemical ecologist from the New Zealand Institute for Plant & Food Research, who was researching 'lure-and-kill' tactics in pest management.

Once lured in, the insect then lands on the leaves and becomes stuck to the mucilage; in its struggle to free itself, it comes into contact with more and more tentacles until it is covered in glue. The more it writhes, the worse its position becomes. The struggling of the insect triggers the outer tentacles, which slowly begin to envelop their prey, curling around the victim and covering it with yet more glue. Eventually the insect's breathing holes become clogged with the sticky substance and it suffocates to death. During this process, the insect is likely to lose a limb, wing or other body part to the struggle, and all in all it can be quite a brutal battle. Less than 20 per cent of insects caught in a drosera's sticky trap make it out alive, and even still, many of those die soon after due to exhaustion or loss of limbs.

The glue which covers the insect's body then gets to work, using acids and enzymes to break down and digest the prey caught within the plant's tentacles. In some species, so much of the digestive fluid is released that it can be seen dripping from the plant, like a drooling animal devouring a tasty meal. The process of digestion can take anywhere from a few hours to a few days, and sometimes, in slower species with larger prey, it can take as long as a week. Because the process can take a while, the sundew also secretes antibacterial compounds, which stop the insect from 'going off' during digestion.

Once all of the insect's insides have been digested, leaving only a shell behind, the sundew's sessile glands get to work absorbing the nutrients provided by the insect. Once absorption is complete, and there are no more nutrients to be obtained from the carcass, the tentacles dry out their glands and begin to uncurl, allowing the shell of the insect to drop from the leaves or be washed away by the rain. Once uncurled, the sundew's leaves then re-secrete the sticky mucilage and wait for their next victim to arrive.

This carnivorous attack, while brutal, allows the sundews to obtain nutrients essential to their survival, and captured insects are perfect for providing them with a burst of life. Sundews use this energy to replace older, tired leaves with fresh, sticky ones, and to produce flowers and seeds for reproduction. In the same way we fertilise our plants, the sundews, too, need food for survival. Without these essential nutrients, the species would quickly become extinct.

DROSERA DOING GOOD

For of all their deceit and digestion methods, drosera may seem cruel, but before you run outside with your trowel to rid the earth of the species, they aren't all bad; in fact, they have been massively beneficial to both ancient and modern medicine.

At least since the 12th century (but perhaps even longer), drosera have been used as a medicinal herb in all countries where they can be found growing naturally. The plant's medicinal value and use varies from species to species, and so it is used to treat different ailments depending on which region it is found growing in. Since the 12th century, in Italy, Germany and other European countries, the plant was used as cough medicine. In India, China and America, sundews were often used to treat skin ailments such as warts and bunions. In Brazil and Mexico, the leaves were crushed and made into tea to treat morning sickness, gastrointestinal upset and other digestive issues.

As we touched on earlier, the leaves and glandular secretions of a sundew contain antibacterial and antimicrobial properties which work to stop the insect or bug the plant has caught from going off while they digest it. The organic compounds which help to prevent this process have proven to be massively beneficial in human healthcare.

There are a great number of organic compounds that make up these antibacterial and antimicrobial effects within the plant, but the two main ones are naphthoquinones (vitamin K) and flavonoids, which have anti-inflammatory properties and are also present in a number of fruits and vegetables. Plumbagin has an antitussive (cough-suppressing) and antispasmodic (spasm-suppressing) effect in humans, which has earned the plant its historical use throughout Europe as a tincture to treat dry coughs, bronchitis, whooping cough, asthma and even tuberculosis. A tea made from the leaves is soothing and has a relaxing effect on throat and respiratory muscles, easing heavy breathing, coughing and wheezing. The sundews are so good at this job that they are still a main ingredient in many over-the-counter cough medicines today.

Ascorbic acid, most commonly referred to as vitamin C, is also present in sundew leaves. Vitamin C is essential to the body and helps with tissue repair and immune system function. It plays a vital role in the healing process, and so can also be massively beneficial for the treatment of chest, throat and gastrointestinal ailments, helping the body to repair itself after the illness has passed.

Since the leaves of a drosera contain enzymes capable of digesting proteins (for insect digestion), the leaves can also be useful for treating skin conditions such as warts, corns and bunions. The leaves, roots and seed heads have also been crushed and applied to the skin to remove freckles and skin abnormalities throughout time.

OTHER USES FOR DROSERA

Aside from tried and tested medicinal value, sundews have also been used for an array of other purposes. *Drosera* were thought to have aphrodisiac qualities, and many Europeans ingested the plant to try and reap the benefits. The supposed effect on humans earned the plant the common name 'lust wort', and although there is no scientific evidence to support the aphrodisiac effects, the tonic was popular across the continent.

Speaking of ingesting drosera, their corms (modified roots) were used by Indigenous peoples in Australia as a food source and were considered a delicacy. They also used the corms as a dye for clothing and other textiles. Many different species of *Drosera* can be found in Australia, and so an array of different-coloured dyes were created using different species' corms. Indigenous Australians also crushed and used the plant as cotton wool due to the viscoelasticity (sticky stretchiness) of the leaves. And in the Scottish Highlands, drosera have been used to dye wool or Harris tweed purple or, when used with ammonia, yellow. Highlanders also used the sundews as rennet to make cheese.

While the sundews have proven their usefulness in both ancient and modern medicine, perhaps the most interesting use of the plant is one that is still being researched by scientists and medical professionals today. Drosera leaves are antibiotic and viscoelastic by nature, and many scientists are using them in tissue engineering as a bioadhesive. As an example, if you were to get some kind of a medical implant, be it a new kidney or a hip replacement, surgeons would use a bioadhesive coating on the implant or organ to help it attach to the surrounding tissue and prevent your body from rejecting it. Drosera is an extremely effective bioadhesive. It allows living tissue to attach and grow on the coating quickly, reducing the risk of rejection, and speeding up recovery time in patients. And due to their antibiotic nature, the risk of infection is greatly reduced when compared to alternatives. Sundews are also easily grown and environmentally friendly to produce, making them a cost-effective choice too.

THE FUTURE'S NOT SO SUNNY

The sundews, once found growing in abundance throughout Europe, are now endangered, nearing critically endangered, in the wild. This is due to the destruction of their habitat: peat bogs. Peat bogs are being diminished throughout Europe, and while there are many 'justifiable' reasons for the harvesting of peat, one which stands out to us the most is that peat is extremely useful as an aggregate in compost. Many peat-free alternatives are now readily available, but peat is still a common component in most, if not all, commercial composts, including compost used by houseplant nurseries through-out Europe. There are countless benefits to the houseplant craze, and growing plants in any shape or form is wonderful for improving mental health and overall well-being in humans. But for the sake of so many of the houseplants we love to grow, we must find better, more sustainable methods of cultivating them. Otherwise, the very market that fuels the trade and our love for the sundews could become responsible for their extinction.

Nepenthes

(pitcher plants or monkey cups)

Native Location
Malay Archipelago

*"Can anyone see such marvellous things, knowing
them only to be plants, and feel no wonder?"*

—— *The Gardeners' Chronicle,*
On Nepenthes, 1849

Nepenthes, also known as pitcher plants or monkey cups, is a genus of carnivorous plants that have been of great interest to botanists, environmentalists and houseplant lovers alike. The intrigue surrounding them and their incredible adaptations have played a major part in attracting us (and many others) to the plant world, namely the existence of a tropical biome that can support plants that eat living things.

The pit-fall traps found within the genus are diverse, and each species has developed its own unique adaptations to attract a great number of different and unfortunate insects, rodents, arthropods and even reptiles – most of whom meet a sticky end.

The majority of species within the *Nepenthes* genus come from the Malay Archipelago and other surrounding tropical regions in South East Asia. And as with many other tropical curiosities, they've become popular as houseplants. They aren't too difficult to keep at home and double up as pest control in the summer months.

Not all species of *Nepenthes* are the same in their trapping

mechanisms, but there are distinct similarities between all of the plants, which ultimately lead to the same end: the harvesting of nutrients.

Nitrogen tends to be the most sought-after nutrient for the pitcher plants, as it is with many other carnivorous plants. Since their natural habitats are often nitrogen-poor, they must find other means of obtaining this all-important nutrient necessary for survival. In this case, the best alternative is to trap and digest insects and animals.

HOW IT WORKS

It can take pitcher plants years to reach true maturity. As they grow, new leaves uncurl from the centre, flattening and growing long and wide, as any other leaf in the plant world would. As the leaf becomes fully formed, the midrib (central vein of the leaf) continues to grow, extending downwards and growing longer, before eventually forming a pitcher.

As the pitcher swells, growing bigger and heavier, it pulls the leaf downwards. In some terrestrial species (those that grow in the earth), the pitcher continues to extend until it reaches the ground where it can be supported. In some epiphytic species (those that grow on other plants and trees), the pitcher grows long and dangles beside or below the plant, drawn down by the force of gravity. Some species of *Nepenthes* are climbers and produce pitchers that both dwell on the ground and dangle beside the plant, up in the canopy. In these instances, both pitchers can look different in colour and shape.

Just before the pitcher reaches full maturity, the lid separates from the rest of the cup, and the peristome (lip) of the pitcher curls over, becoming a ribbed and slippery landing for insects and animals. When the pitcher is fully formed, it can resemble a rounded cup or a champagne flute.

The rim, lid and walls of the pitcher can be extremely waxy and slippery, and climbing or landing on them is often what gets their victims in trouble. *Nepenthes* draw insects, small mammals and other animals in by secreting (an often sweet-smelling) nectar via glands on the lids of the pitchers. The lid of the pitcher can be concave and soft or rubbery and rigid.

The lid also acts like a kind of umbrella, stopping too much rainwater from falling in. This would not only dilute the solution within the pitcher and make digesting prey difficult but could also cause an overflow, washing any captured prey out of the pitcher completely.

In many species of *Nepenthes*, a rigid lid paired with a nectar-covered underside work hand in hand during the rainy season to increase the number of prey captured. When a raindrop hits the top of the rigid lid and causes reverberation, any ants or other insects feeding from the nectar find it impossible to grip on and drop into the pitcher.

The pitcher itself is filled with a concentrated, viscoelastic fluid full of digestive enzymes, which is secreted from glands at the base of the cup. This fluid is present even before the lid separates from the rest of the pitcher. It's essential in the digestion and absorption of nutrients from fallen victims. The strength of the solution varies from species to species, but some pitchers can contain fluid with a pH balance as low as two (the same acidity as lemon juice), while others are less acidic, with a more neutral pH balance of around six (roughly the same as milk or urine).

When animals and insects fall into the digestive fluid of the pitcher, they drown and then their corpses are digested by the acidic enzymes in the pitcher. Finally, the nutrients from their bodies are absorbed and distributed throughout the plant.

DIFFERENT PITCHERS
AND THEIR METHODS

Not all species of *Nepenthes* have the same prey in mind when forming their characteristic pitchers, and not all of them rely of the consumption of drowned animals and insects. We think the following pitchers are some of the most interesting, both in terms of adaptations and of prey.

Nepenthes rajah

Nepenthes rajah is a wonderful example of one species that's found an effective way of maximising nutrient uptake from visiting animals. *N. rajah* is a terrestrial carnivore and mostly produces pitchers which rest on the ground or against a supporting object, such as a rock. This is essential to the plant since it has the capability of producing some of the largest pitchers found in the entire genus. They can grow to be 40 cm (15½ in) in length, with the capacity to hold up to 2.5 litres (87½ fl oz) of digestive fluid in one pitcher alone. The pitchers are stout (short and wide) compared to others' and have a much less slippery rim.

Considering this description, you might be wondering what kind of animal this plant is capable of capturing. But it is not necessarily what the plant is able to catch, but more about how the plant utilises the size of its pitchers to achieve the greatest results. *N. rajah* is not entirely reliant on insects, as many other species of *Nepenthes* are. Instead, it looks to the humble tree shrew for most of its nutrients and does so without turning it into a meal.

The tree shrew stands to benefit a lot from its visit to the pitcher, since the lid secretes an abundance of sweet-smelling nectar to feed from. The lid itself is also one of the largest of all *Nepenthes'* lids and is positioned in such a way that the shrew can only access the nectar on the underside of the concave lid by squatting over the opening to the pitcher. *N. rajah's* non-slip rim supports the weight of the shrew, allowing it to sit and lick the nectar-covered rim for hours upon hours until it has had its fill. The space between the mouth and the lid of the pitcher is also the perfect distance for the shrew to squat comfortably while feeding.

Over the course of a few hours, while the tree shrew is licking up all the nectar, it pays its dues in the form of excrement, which it deposits directly into the opening of the pitcher. This may seem like an unfair exchange, but the tree shrew's droppings are high in essential nutrients which the plant needs to survive.

But life could still prove to be difficult if *N. rajah* relied solely on tree shrew droppings for survival, reproduction and nectar production, and it would have to produce a great deal of nectar to keep the hungry animal satisfied. Studies have found that this species also has a similar relationship with another mammal: the summit rat. While tree shrews are most likely to visit the plants during the day, the nocturnal summit rat stops by at night, repeating the same process as the tree shrew and leaving its droppings as payment.

As with many other pitcher plants, *N. rajah* also captures insects like ants and centipedes, and sometimes extends its palate to animals further up the food chain, digesting small vertebrates like frogs and lizards. On occasion, summit rats and tree shrews have been found drowned within the pitchers, although this is likely due to a mistake in footing on the part of the victims, rather than the purposeful carnivory of the plant.

Nepenthes hemsleyana

Shaped like an elegant, elongated champagne flute, the pitchers of *Nepenthes hemsleyana* support the roosting of woolly bats, who seek out the 'best-shaped' roost using echolocation. The mouth, the lid and shape of the pitcher support 'echo-reflection', which means the bat is able to locate the pitcher, judge its shape and size (discerning it from other pitcher plants), and roost comfortably for the night.

The pitcher itself is the perfect size for woolly bats, who rarely grow to be bigger than an adorable 4 cm (1.5 in). The pitcher is snug but can also act as a sleeping bag for more than one bat at a time if necessary (provided the bats are willing to share). While the bat is roosting, it pays its dues in the form of excrement, feeding the plant and allowing the mutualistic relationship to continue.

While the pitcher is ideal in size for the woolly bat, there are a few other factors which make *N. hemsleyana* the perfect hotel for the night. The digestive fluid, for example, only fills the very bottom of the pitcher, and never reaches the middle or top section where the bat roosts, meaning it can enjoy a peaceful night's sleep without fear of being slowly digested.

Another interesting feature is its waxy inside walls. The walls of some other species' pitchers (which the bats could opt to roost in instead) support the laying of arthropod eggs, larvae or pupae, which are parasitic and can make the bats sick (like a hostel with a bedbug infestation). Since the walls of *N. hemsleyana* are slippery, and do not support the laying of eggs, larvae or pupae, the bats can roost without worrying about sharing their bed with parasitic chancers.

Nepenthes khasiana

Nepenthes khasiana is extremely endangered and is the only species of *Nepenthes* found growing in India – more specifically, it is endemic to the Khasi Hills in Meghalaya. The species grows as a large terrestrial shrub, with pitchers ranging between 10 cm (4 in) and 20 cm (8 in) long.

While the pitcher is unremarkable in its prey (catching mainly ants and other insects) and, to the eye, it resembles the standard shape and form of any pitcher plant, the biology behind *N. khasiana* is unique and perhaps the most interesting of all the plants listed here. The Khasi people call the plant *tiew rakot*, which roughly translates to 'demon flower' – a name not given lightly.

The main lure for its prey is the glowing fluorescent-blue rim of the pitcher. To the human eye, it's unnoticeable, but once it's placed under UV light it's unmistakable. Since UV light is visible to insects, the rim is enticing, perhaps resembling a flower with an abundance of nectar. One study has suggested that the rim emits the most powerful glow of any plant species anywhere on earth.

As well as its glow, *N. khasiana* uses another unique method to lure in its prey: carbon dioxide emissions. As each individual pitcher matures, and the lid lifts off the rim, the pitcher begins to emit CO_2 – a sign of a potential food source to an insect. The insect is first lured in by the gas and the rim confirms to it that there is a delicious food source nearby. Then, as seen in many other species of *Nepenthes*, upon inspecting the pitcher, the insect slips on the rim and falls into the digestive fluid.

The CO_2 produced by *N. khasiana* doesn't just lure prey into its trap; carbon dioxide has been found within the digestive fluid of the pitcher as well, both aiding the plant in digestion and helping to tranquilise any prey trapped in the fluid.

Another mechanism utilised by *N. khasiana* which is unique to the genus is its creation and secretion of antifungal compounds into the fluid of the pitcher. When the pitcher matures, and CO_2 is released, the insect is lured in. When the first-ever insect is captured, it acts as a trigger, and the plant releases antifungal compounds into the fluid — avoiding any unnecessary infections or diseases from being absorbed by the pitcher. For this reason, many Khasi people harvest the pitchers for the treatment of infections and diseases, unfortunately contributing to the rarity of the species.

THE POWERS OF DIGESTION

From the bat hotel to the seemingly radioactive pitcher, *Nepenthes* species have long been the subject of excitement and intrigue for botanists and plant enthusiasts alike, with the discovery of each new species opening up a whole world of study. Observing the way *Nepenthes* and other carnivorous plants have adapted to unfavourable environments has broadened our understanding of plant evolution, and yet we still have much to learn from them.

If you are like us, and the child-like image of *Nepenthes* conjures up a triffid-esque, man-eating, belching carnivore, then you already have the fascination it takes to immerse yourself into the world of carnivorous plants. Growing them for yourself at home, learning about them and observing them and their unique behaviours only serves to deepen the fascination further.

Counting Carnivores

When considering carnivorous plants, the first that comes to mind is usually *Dionaea muscipula*, most commonly known as a Venus flytrap. Their small but menacing jaws and pink insides are characteristic of what we might imagine a meat-eating plant to look like – but there is much more than meets the eye when it comes to this inspiring plant.

WHAT'S IN A NAME?

Native to North and South Carolina, USA, where copperhead snakes, alligators, venomous water vipers and gigantic tarantulas are easily found, this carnivore fits in perfectly. You'll find them growing in sunny peat bogs, swamps and flooded savannahs among sphagnum moss, where nitrogen and phosphorous levels in the sandy soil are low. Wildfires are common in these areas, and Venus flytraps rely on the occurrence to keep their habitat open and any competition at bay. As with the other carnivorous plants we've discussed in this book, Venus flytraps rely on insects to provide them with the nutrients they need to survive in such nutrient-deficient landscapes. Unlike sticky flypaper traps like drosera (page 132), from which they evolved, dionaea like to eat beetles, spiders and other crawling insects that can't easily fly away and have a much greater nutritional value than most flying insects.

The names associated with this fly-catcher are no accident. Their common name 'Venus' is in reference to the Roman goddess of love, while '*Dionaea*', their Latin genus name, means daughter of 'Dione' – and refers to the Greek goddess of love, Aphrodite. It is a wonder that such an unromantic, swamp-dwelling carnivore would be named after not one but two amorous goddesses. But in Greek

CHAPTER 6: CARNIVORES

and Roman mythology, Venus and Aphrodite are tricksters who use their beauty to beguile and trap men to help them do their bidding. Making a bit more sense now?

Another possible reason for their names is the way their traps look; it is thought that the plant may have been named after the female goddesses because of their open, pinkish-red jaws, which, according to those who first discovered the plant, bear a passing resemblance to female genitalia. The plant's species name is much more straightforward – with *muscipula* in Latin simply meaning 'flytrap'.

While a necessity in any exotic plant collector's glasshouse, Venus flytraps have become increasingly common as a house and tender (frost-sensitive) potted garden plant among the general population over the last decade or two. With the rise in popularity of carnivorous plants in popular culture (think Audrey II in the 1986 film *Little Shop of Horrors*), they're relatively easy to get hold of. And an increase in common knowledge of the once-elusive plants means that they're becoming easier to grow at home as well. But perhaps the most enticing component of a Venus flytrap is the same component that sees small children poking at the plant with sticks and fingers, eager to observe the outcome: its snap-trapping jaws.

MIND YOUR FINGERS

Venus flytraps belong to a small group of plants with trigger-fast reactive movements, which includes *Mimosa pudica* (page 110) and *Drosera* (page 132). These rapid movements are what make dionaea so successful as a carnivorous plant, and other highly evolved mechanisms within the plant mean they don't waste too much energy in the process.

As with other carnivorous plants, Venus flytraps start their process by luring in their prey. They begin with their best asset and their most attractive feature to an insect: their colour. The pinkish red of the inside of their snap-trap resembles a flower and promises a nectar reward to those who visit. But the colour of the trap alone is not enough to attract a nutritional meal, and so the carnivore secretes a complex blend of sweet-smelling VOCs (volatile organic compounds) from glands inside of its pink 'mouth'. These trick its prey into thinking there are fruit and flower rewards in store. In many instances, this delicious scent will be the first attractant, while the pink colouring confirms the source for the crawling insect. Venus flytraps tend to attract insects like beetles, spiders and other arthropods, such as ants and grasshoppers, rather than winged insects – this is ideal for the snap-trap, as flying insects are difficult to keep around for long enough to successfully ensnare once they realise they've been fooled.

The modified leaves are split into two halves, similarly to a clam, and joined in the middle by what would have been the midrib (central vein) of the leaf. The outer edges are covered in cilia – the characteristic tooth-like hairs that stop larger insects from escaping before the trap snaps all the way shut, while allowing smaller insects to escape through the 'bars' of the prison. This way, the plant doesn't waste too much energy producing digestive enzymes for an insignificant meal. Both halves of the modified leaf are concave when open (curved inwards), and when the trap is activated, it seemingly snaps closed to become convex (curving outwards).

The inner part of the trap is covered in small hairs, known as 'trigger hairs'. Once the insect is attracted, it climbs onto the modified leaves and brushes past the trigger hairs on the inside of the trap. Once the hairs are activated, the trap quickly snaps shut, hermetically sealing the unfortunate insect inside where it writhes around until the trap fills up with a soup full of digestive enzymes – drowning the insect and, eventually, consuming it.

The time between the snapping shut of the trap to the reopening can take between five and 12 days. Once the trap has absorbed all possible nutrients from its prey, it reopens and the empty husk of the insect is either washed away in the rain or blown off by the wind. This process can be pretty taxing, and so after five or so captures of prey, the individual trap will wilt and die – only to be replaced by a new, younger trap.

COUNTING CARNIVORES

Interestingly, if a trigger hair is only stimulated once, the trap remains open – this stops the plant from wasting precious energy snapping its leaves shut when there's no nutritional value to be gained. But things aren't quite as simple as that. Rainer Hedrich, a biophysicist who has studied dionaea and their mechanisms of operation in depth, has surmised that the plants can not only count to five but also store memories, much like the bashful *Mimosa pudica* (page 110). He found that flytraps use a complex mechanism of calcium signals, alongside their specialised, hinged trigger hairs, to create a chain reaction of events when catching their prey.

First, the insect crawls onto the plant; once it reaches the inside of the trap, it stimulates a trigger hair. This stimulation triggers a massive peak in calcium that runs throughout the plant, a bit like an electrical current. If only one trigger hair is stimulated within 30 seconds or so, the calcium reaches its peak and then falls back to normal levels within the plant, and no action is taken. This might be the result of a bit of falling debris, a raindrop, or a flying insect that didn't hang around. In this way, a Venus flytrap stores the memory of the stimulation until it is no longer useful – if there is no further stimulation past this point, the calcium levels within the plant return to the starting point within 60 seconds.

However, if a second trigger hair is stimulated within 30 seconds of the first, the two signals overlap and send the calcium levels soaring, which sees the once convex leaf halves shut. This can happen in one-tenth of a second – faster than the blink of an eye. Once the trap is sealed with the insect inside, the insect writhes around in a desperate bid to escape its newfound prison. As the insect writhes around, it stimulates even more trigger hairs, sending more and more signals flying throughout the plant. The more trigger hairs are stimulated, the more digestive enzymes are prepared, since this appears to be proof of larger prey. A cricket can stimulate an average of 63 trigger hairs in an hour – and so the plant produces a more concentrated concoction to be sure the insect is digested properly.

"Obviously it doesn't have a brain to go 'one, two, three, four' ... Effectively, it's counting. It's just not thinking about it."

—

Wayne Fagerberg,
Professor of molecular,
cellular and biomedical
sciences at the University
of New Hampshire

Once the trigger hairs have been stimulated five times, the Venus flytrap begins to secrete digestive fluid and enzymes. The fluid fills the stomach-like cavity and digests the insect – and the enzymes reabsorb the nutrient-laden soup.

So what's the significance of lucky number five? Well, it is still possible that fallen debris could stimulate two trigger hairs at once, activating the snap-trap. If this happens, but the stimulation doesn't continue, calcium levels within the plant slowly decrease back to a normal level. In that case, no energy-sapping digestive enzymes are secreted. Instead, the flytrap reopens within a few days to rid itself of the time-wasting debris and lie in wait for something more promising to stop by. But if three more trigger hairs are stimulated, it knows it's in for a decent meal.

THE AFTERMATH

If we consider 'intelligence' in a capacity other than our own, plants are most likely, if not definitely, capable of it. And if this is so, then surely *Dionaea muscipula* is a worthy candidate of the title of world's smartest plant. Whether, consciously or unconsciously, the ability to count is a standard by which we do measure human intelligence, and the ability to count down to the release of signals to perform an action even more so. If this was the only argument in favour of a Venus flytrap's higher intelligence, it could be more easily ignored. But the plant also uses this method to distinguish between debris and prey, as well as the size and therefore nutritional value of the captured prey – all to stop itself from wasting precious time, energy and nutrients.

Although they've gained massive popularity, and are regularly cultivated in plant nurseries, Venus flytraps are becoming increasingly more endangered in the wild, with the expansion of urban areas in their natural habitats leading to the destruction of peat bogs and wet savannahs in both North and South Carolina. Over 70 per cent of flytrap habitat prevalent in the 1970s has now been developed, and where you might once have found flytraps, alligators and peat bogs all creating a wonderful ecosystem, it is now more common to come across golf courses, car parks and supermarkets. To reduce the risk of damage to their new infrastructure, humans have taken measures to prevent the lightning strikes that lead to wildfires. But the lack of wildfires means trees and other plants are able to flourish, impacting Venus flytrap habitats. Alongside these two, very real threats, poachers known as 'flytrappers' uproot the plants from protected areas in their native habitats, where conservationists try desperately to keep them as a treasured member of the eco-system. What's more insulting is that the poachers often sell the plants for no more than 18 pence (25 cents), and only face a £70 ($100) fine for stealing entire communities of flytraps.

Does this all mean we should never keep a Venus flytrap as a houseplant? Well, no. It just means, as with many other species of endangered plants, we should try and be wary of where our plants come from and make sure they are grown responsibly – without adding to the destruction of the plant's native habitat. Buy small from local nurseries, check with your providers that the plants are grown responsibly, and most of all, enjoy having this wonderfully complex carnivore as a house guest.

Published in 2021 by Hardie Grant Books,
an imprint of Hardie Grant Publishing

Hardie Grant Books (London)
5th & 6th Floors
52–54 Southwark Street
London SE1 1UN

Hardie Grant Books (Melbourne)
Building 1, 658 Church Street
Richmond, Victoria 3121

hardiegrantbooks.com

Text © Maddie Bailey and Alice Bailey
Illustrations © Lucy Rose

British Library Cataloguing-in-Publication Data.
A catalogue record for this book is available from
the British Library.

The Hidden Histories of Houseplants
ISBN: 978-1-78488-405-5

10 9 8 7 6 5 4 3

Publisher: Kajal Mistry
Commissioning Editor: Eve Marleau
Editor: Eila Purvis
Design and Art Direction: Stuart Hardie
Illustrations: Lucy Rose
Copy-editor: Sarah Herman
Proofreader: Meredith Olson
Indexer: Cathy Heath
Production Controller: Katie Jarvis

Colour reproduction by p2d
Printed and bound in China by Leo Paper Products Ltd.

Acknowledgements

We would like to thank Eve and Eila at Hardie Grant: Eve for helping us to develop and form our ideas until they became book-worthy, and Eila for giving us this opportunity and mentoring, guiding and supporting us throughout the whole process, and ensuring this book fits with our visions. Their process and help has been invaluable and we couldn't have done it without them.

To Stuart, our designer, and Lucy Rose, our illustrator, who gave our book life. Thank you for making it so beautiful!

We want to say a huge thank you to the entire team at Forest (Thea, Ella, Flora, Anastasia, Hannah, Emily, Lou, Joe, Lucy and James) for holding fort and encouraging us while we took the time to write, and for the endless sharing of knowledge and tips, and the general natter about plants, which has helped to deepen our combined understanding of the ever-expanding houseplant world.

A massive thank you to our whole family for introducing us to the world of horticulture and encouraging us to do what we love. To Dad (Keith) for encouraging us to pursue our dreams and to Thea for keeping us entertained when we needed some light relief, and for always being there for us.

Finally, to our Mum, Fran. Your experience and knowledge has brought us to where we are today – we are so grateful for the opportunities you have given us, and for your help and guidance both in life and throughout our horticultural careers.